Lebanese Cuisine

More than 185 Simple,

Delicious Authentic Recipes

MADELAIN FARAH &
LEILA HABIB-KIRSKE

Hatherleigh Press is committed to preserving and protecting the natural resources of the earth. Environmentally responsible and sustainable practices are embraced within the company's mission statement.

Visit us at www.hatherleighpress.com.

Lebanese Cuisine

Text copyright © 1972, 1974, 1979, 1982, 1985, 2023

by Madelain Farah & Leila Habib-Kirske

Library of Congress Cataloging-in-Publication Data is available upon request.

ISBN: 978–1-57826–949-5

Cover and Interior Design by Carolyn Kasper

Photography by Leila Habib-Kirske and Chad Lund (Lund Digital Media, LLC)

Printed in the United States

10 9 8 7 6 5 4 3 2 1

To my mother

*If you bake bread with indifference, you bake a
bitter bread that feeds but half man's hunger.*

—KAHLIL GIBRAN

Contents

Preface

THIS EDITION CELEBRATES THE 50-year anniversary of the original
publication of *Lebanese Cuisine* authored by Madelain Farah. Looking back at
the original book, it was a quaint affair—spiral bound, no pictures with a handful
of drawings. That said, it was representative of its time. Beyond its simplicity, it
resonated within the Middle Eastern community and beyond, selling over 100,000
copies by the early 2000s. I cannot tell you how many times I ran into a person
who said that either they or a family member had a worn-out copy on their kitchen
counter. These individuals were from cities across the U.S., into Europe and
beyond. It is a testament to the authenticity of the work.

Lebanese cooking as represented in this book is very much aligned with trends
in cooking today with lower use of meats, vegetarian and vegan options. The cuisine
weighs heavily on vegetables with a focus on eating with the season, aligning with
farm to table and local produce movements. Pita bread, tabbouleh and hummus
have become so popular that they have lost their association with their originating
culture. Recipes have been adjusted in minor ways, either to correct a recipe that
has been found to be a little off, or to clarify seasoning. For example, using kosher
salt rather than table salt. Personally, I find that my taste today tends toward stron-
ger seasoning, so I will use a slightly heavier hand in certain recipes—or even add a
pinch of red pepper flakes. As you cook, feel free to do the same.

A tremendous thank you to my friend and collaborator on the photography,
Chad Lund. An exceptional wildlife photographer, he took on the challenge with
me (an analog black and white street photographer) to photograph the recipes for
the book.

My mother wrote this book to memorialize the recipes of my grandmother. The idea to do so was prompted by a scolding from her father. After moving to Washington D.C. and not having learned to cook, she would call her mother collect to ask how one dish or another was prepared. After one too many expensive phone bills, her father had enough. He said, "Either you learn to cook, or you pay for your own phone calls!"

Twenty years later, she set out to write this book. Ingredients were literally captured as my grandmother would throw them into the pot. Recipes were documented, tested, and re-tested so that they would capture the nuances of the old-school cook: "how does it look" or "take a piece and smell for seasonings" or "test for the temperature with your thumb." As a little girl, I watched the entire process, and was an eager taster.

This is the how-to for preparation of soul-warming Lebanese foods, which are passed down from generation to generation. Many of us associate joy with the foods of our childhood, many stemming from our ethnic roots. To me, the fondest memories are of my grandmother baking bread. She would make a tiny loaf just for me. I would wait impatiently as it baked, then enjoy it, warm from the oven, dipped in a bit of olive oil. From my mother and grandmother, I learned both the skill and the creative pleasure of home cooking. Today, the most cherished item in my kitchen is an American earthenware bowl that my grandmother used to prepare everything from blueberry pancakes to *laban*.

I hope that you enjoy this book and that it will bring new traditions to your table.

—Leila Habib-Kirske

Introduction

Lebanon. The land of the Phoenicians—a mosaic of peoples, cultures, mores, and customs; of religions and costumes; crossroads of spice routes and civilizations: all epitomized today in modern Lebanon, a country that still conveys the flavor of the past. This book introduces the art of Lebanese cuisine—recipes that are representative of the Middle East as a whole. While I may be cooking in a modern American kitchen, the aroma of the Lebanese kitchen is the same here as it was for my mother and grandmother in Lebanon.

In the Middle East, not unlike in many other cultures, the chief cook in an extended family is queen of her home, and her throne is essentially in the kitchen. No sooner is breakfast done, than preparation for lunch has begun, and then again for dinner. It takes a measure of oneself in cooking that goes far beyond the measured ingredients. Mealtime in the Middle East is a leisurely and a happy occasion, during which the family is brought together in thanksgiving and mirth.

The time has come, however, when "a pinch of this," or "a little of that," and the "come-and-watch-me" technique of generation upon generation of daughters observing mothers is no longer feasible for the modern mobile family, or for the conscientious cook with limited time to spend in the kitchen. My aim here has been to put down on paper what I learned in the kitchen of my mother.

Recipe Titles and Spellings

Arabic titles are given along with their English translations. Though there are many local variations for these recipes, with slight changes in ingredients, the names are basically the same.

Colloquial rather than classical Arabic is used in the transliteration of these names. While in most cases the spelling represents sounds that are very similar to those existing in English, the following is a brief description of the symbols, which do not exist in the English alphabet, together with a brief description of the sounds they represent: vowel length and hard consonants are not indicated; is a glottal stop, which is pronounced like a tin ask; is a pharyngeal variation of the a produced by drawing the tongue as far back into the throat as possible and blowing through the narrow passage in the pharynx; gb represents a sound similar to the French r; kb is pronounced like the ch in Bach. The foregoing explanation of sounds should help the cook pronounce the names somewhat accurately.

Typically, Arabic-speaking people say *sahtayn* upon completion of a meal. It literally means "two healths to you." May you enjoy many happy hours of cooking and sahtayn.

—Madelain Farah

While most of the ingredients in this book can be readily bought any-where, there are some ingredients, especially some spices, that might be harder to find. You should be able to find these in Middle Eastern grocery stores, specialty shops, or online.

Bharat	Purslane Purslane
Burma (or Knafi) Dough	Rawbi
Kishk	Sahlab
Mahlab	Sumac
Mistka	Za'atar
Mlukhiyyi	

THE RECIPES

Sauces

Tahini is a staple of Middle Eastern and Mediterranean cooking. A paste made from toasted ground hulled sesame seeds, it is a key ingredient in hummus, baba ghanoush, sauces and halva. Tahini is vegan and gluten free.

Previously an obscure and exotic ingredient, tahini is now widely available in grocery stores and specialty markets. As an ingredient, it adds richness, depth and nuttiness. When combined with lemon and water, it becomes creamy and pourable.

In this section, tahini is used as a base for sauces. Upon opening a jar or can, stir the tahini well, as the oil has usually separated. Tahini keeps indefinitely without refrigeration.

HINTS

- When making a sauce with tahini, always blend water with the tahini first, then add the lemon juice. This makes for a whiter sauce.

Tahini Sauce

Taratur

MAKES 4–6 SERVINGS

1 clove garlic
1 teaspoon kosher salt
½ cup tahini
½ cup water
½ cup lemon juice

Mash the garlic and salt together. Add the tahini, mixing well. The sauce will thicken. Gradually add the water, blending thoroughly. Then add the lemon juice. Blend well.

NOTE: This can be a thin or thick sauce, depending upon use and preference. Simply adjust with lemon juice and water. This can be used with vegetables or in combination with other recipes.

Parsley in Tahini Sauce

Baqdunis bit-Tahini

MAKES 4–6 SERVINGS

1 clove garlic
1 teaspoon kosher salt
½ cup tahini
½ cup water
½ cup lemon juice
½ cup parsley,
    coarsely chopped

Mash the garlic and the salt together. Add the tahini, mixing thoroughly. The sauce will thicken as you stir. Gradually add the water, softening the mixture. Add the lemon juice, blending well. Gently stir in the parsley.

NOTE: This is especially good as an appetizer dip or served with grilled fish.

Garlic Sauce

Tum biz-Zayt

MAKES 6–8 SERVINGS

3 cloves garlic, minced
½ cup olive oil
¼ cup lemon juice
Salt to taste

Mix all of the ingredients well.

NOTE: This goes well with broiled or grilled chicken. To eat, dip the chicken in the sauce. Garlic sauce can also be used to brush chicken while broiling or grilling—just thin with more lemon juice.

Yogurt Sauce

Salsat al-Laban

MAKES 6 SERVINGS

1 egg or 1 tablespoon
  cornstarch
1 quart yogurt
1⅓ cups water
2 teaspoons kosher salt

In a pan, beat the egg well with a fork. (If you're using cornstarch, first dissolve it in ½ cup of cold water before blending it with the yogurt.) Add the yogurt and water, blending thoroughly for at least 5 minutes.

Place the pan on a medium flame and stir constantly with a wooden spoon in one direction for 20 minutes or until the sauce comes to a boil. This mixture may curdle or scorch if not watched carefully. Add the salt and continue cooking for a few more minutes.

NOTE: This is usually served with the Kibbi in Yogurt Sauce (page 133).

Yogurt Sauce with Mint

Laban bin-Na'na'

MAKES 6 SERVINGS

1 large clove garlic

3 tablespoons fresh chopped mint
   or 1 tablespoon crushed dried mint

¼ cup butter

1 egg or 1 tablespoon cornstarch

1 quart yogurt

1⅓ cups water

Salt to taste

Mash the garlic, mint, and salt together. Sauté in butter and set aside.

In a pan, beat the egg well with a fork. If you are using cornstarch, first dissolve it in ½ cup of cold water before blending it with the yogurt. Add the yogurt and water, blending thoroughly for at least 5 minutes. Place on a medium flame and stir constantly with a wooden spoon in one direction.

After 10 minutes, add the mint mixture and continue stirring in one direction only for 10 minutes more.

NOTE: This is usually served with Lamb Supreme with Yogurt (page 214), Stuffed Lamb Delicacies in Yogurt Sauce (page 216), or Stuffed Zucchini (page 146).

Bread & Bread Dishes

There are many names for, and forms of Arabic bread: *kmaj, marquq, tlami, saj, furn*. Some are made thick (*tlami*), others paper-thin (*saj*); some are cooked over a metal dome on an open fire, some baked in ovens. However, the basic Arabic bread recipe is used for all of these variations. It is a trick as well as an art to be able to cook good Arabic bread. In the Middle East, a woman would set aside one day for making bread and bread dishes, all of which require the basic dough recipe. However, with the conveniences of modern life, bread can be made much more quickly and easily.

HINTS

- While making the basic Arabic bread recipe, dip your hands in water when kneading to give a smooth elastic finish to the dough.
- Where ground lamb is required, ground chuck or ground round may be substituted.

Definitions of Arabic Breads

Kmaj: Round flat bread with a pocket used for sandwiches, dips, Arabic pizzas, and so forth.

Marquq: Very thin, round, flat bread, rolled like Italian pizza dough.

Tlami: Round, flat, soft-textured, thick bread without a pocket used for *mnaqish* and as regular bread.

Saj: Paper-thin bread that is baked over a metal dome on an open fire.

Furn: Term used for Arabic bread made commercially.

Arabic Bread: Basic Bread Dough

Khubz 'Arabi

MAKES 7–9 LOAVES

1 package of active
  dry yeast
1 tablespoon sugar
2 cups lukewarm water
6 cups flour
2 teaspoons kosher salt
⅓ cup milk

Dissolve the yeast and sugar in ½ cup of the warm water. Let stand 5–10 minutes. Place the flour and salt in a large bowl, making a depression in the center. Combine the remaining water, milk, and dissolved yeast; pour it into the depression. Begin mixing the flour with the liquid, making sure all batter on the sides of the bowl is worked into the dough. Knead until a smooth dough results and the sides of the bowl are clean. (Hands are occasionally dipped in more water while kneading to give a smooth, elastic finish.)

Cover the dough with a towel and let rise in a warm place until it doubles in size (2–4 hours). Grab orange-size balls from the edge of the dough and form into smooth balls until all the dough is used. Cover the dough balls with a cotton kitchen towel and let rise on another cloth towel for 30 minutes. Roll the balls into ¼-inch-thick circles. Cover and let rise again on a cloth for 30 minutes.

Heat the oven to 475°F. Place the dough directly on racks in the oven. As soon as the dough puffs into a mound, 2–5 minutes, place it under the broiler for few seconds until it is lightly browned. Cool.

NOTE: Many of the recipes that follow are made with this basic dough. The dough freezes well.

Seasoned Flat Tart

Mnaqish biz-Za'atar

MAKES 2 TARTS

2 loaves of unbaked Arabic bread dough

4 tablespoons za'atar

4 tablespoons olive oil

1–2 teaspoon lemon juice, optional, depending on tartness desired

Prepare the Arabic bread dough, and just prior to baking set aside 2 loaves for mnaqish. Mix the za'atar well with the oil and lemon. Roll the dough into a ½-inch-thick circle. Flute the edges.

Pour the oil and lemon mixture evenly on the dough and smooth it over the surface, pressing it gently with 4 fingers, leaving finger impressions on the dough. Place the dough on a lightly greased pizza or cookie sheet. Bake at 475°F for about 8 minutes or until golden brown.

NOTE: The oil in the mixture may be slightly increased or decreased depending on desired thickness of sauce. Za'atar is a spice mixture that is available in Middle Eastern specialty stores or online.

Arabic Cheese Pizza

Khubz bij-Jibneh

MAKES 1 PIZZA

1 individual pita bread
3 slices of cheese
½ fresh tomato, sliced
¼ teaspoon oregano

Open the pocket of pita from the side, leaving half of the circle attached. Arrange the slices of cheese, followed by slices of tomatoes, and top with a sprinkling of oregano. Close the top.

Bake at 350°F until the cheese is melted.

NOTE: This is perfect for a snack or lunch.

Spinach Triangle Pies
Sbanikh bil-'Ajin

MAKES 3–4 DOZEN PIES

FILLING

2 bunches of fresh
   spinach
1 bunch of green
   onions
1 medium onion
⅛ teaspoon allspice
½ cup olive oil
¾–1 cup lemon juice
1 pomegranate,
   shelled, optional
1 cup raisins, optional
Salt and pepper
   to taste

CRUST

1 Arabic Bread dough
   recipe (page 13)

Wash the greens and drain well. Finely chop the spinach, green onions, and onion. To the onions, add the allspice, salt, and pepper and work with your fingers, then mix well with the green onions and spinach, adding the oil and lemon juice. Add either pomegranate or raisins, *but not both*. If pomegranate is used, reduce the amount of lemon juice to ½ cup.

Working quickly, roll the dough like a piecrust to roughly ¼ inch in thickness. Cut it into 4-inch rounds. Place a heaping tablespoon of the filling on each round and wrap the dough closed in the shape of a triangle.

Grease the bottom of a baking sheet with oil and place the pies in rows. Bake at 400°F until golden brown.

NOTE: When closing the pies, be careful not to get juices on the edges. This will make it difficult to close. If need be, however, dip fingers in flour and close.

NOTE: Shortcut alternatives to using basic bread dough are defrosted bread roll dough such as Rhodes Yeast Dinner Rolls or refrigerated tube biscuits. Just flatten and fill.

Triangle Meat Pies

Ftayir

MAKES 20–25 PIES

FILLING

1 pound ground lamb or beef

2 medium onions, finely chopped

½ cup pine nuts

⅛ teaspoon cinnamon

Salt and pepper to taste

CRUST

½ Arabic Bread dough recipe, 3–4 balls of dough

Lemon, cut into wedges (optional)

Thoroughly mix all of the filling ingredients. After the dough has risen for 30 minutes, roll each ball as for a thick piecrust and cut them into 3–4-inch rounds. (Reroll the leftover pieces.) Place a tablespoon of filling on each round and spread it to within ½-inch of the edges. Pinch the edges closed to form a triangle, leaving a small hole in the center in order for the meat to cook. Place the triangles closely together on a well-greased baking sheet.

Bake at 400°F for about 20 minutes or until golden brown. These may be served with lemon wedges, which can be squeezed into the center opening of each ftayir.

NOTE: Shortcut alternatives to using basic bread dough are defrosted bread roll dough such as Rhodes Yeast Dinner Rolls or refrigerated tube biscuits. Just flatten and fill. If the dough seems dry and difficult to seal, lightly dip your fingers in water and seal. Ftayir may be frozen.

Open Faced Patties

Sfiha or *Lahm bil-'Ajin*

MAKES 2–3 DOZEN

FILLING

1 pound ground lamb
    or beef

1 large onion, finely
    chopped

½ cup pine nuts

⅛ teaspoon cinnamon

1 cup yogurt or
    1 tablespoon
    lemon juice

Salt and pepper
    to taste

CRUST

½ Arabic Bread dough
    recipe, 3–4 balls
    of dough

Thoroughly mix the filling ingredients, adding the yogurt or lemon juice last. After the dough has risen, roll each ball as for a piecrust to roughly ¼ inch thickness and cut into 3-inch rounds. Flute the edges. Spread a tablespoon of the filling evenly on each individual round.

Place the patties close together on a greased baking sheet. Bake at 375°F for 20–25 minutes or until golden brown.

NOTE: Yogurt or lemon juice may be omitted from the filling.

Pepper Patties

Ftayir bil-Flayfli

MAKES 2–3 DOZEN

FILLING

1 cup diced red sweet
   peppers
1 medium onion,
   grated
½ cup chopped
   walnuts
½ teaspoon salt
½ teaspoon pepper
Juice of half a lemon
Olive oil to soften
   mixture

CRUST

½ Arabic Bread dough
   recipe (page 13)

Mix all the filling ingredients. Adjust the olive oil so the mixture is the consistency of a thick sauce. After the bread dough has risen, roll it as for a piecrust and cut it into 3-inch rounds. Flute the edge. Evenly spread a heaping teaspoon of the filling on the individual rounds, pressing the filling gently into the dough. Place the patties close together on a greased baking sheet.

Bake at 425°F for 15 minutes or until the pastry is browned.

NOTE: All of the filling ingredients may be coarsely ground in a food processor. Green peppers may be substituted for red peppers, or a combination of both.

Holy Bread

Qurban

MAKES 1 LOAF

1 package of yeast

1 tablespoon sugar

1⅓ cups
   lukewarm water

6 cups flour

½ teaspoon kosher salt

½ teaspoon mahlab,
   finely ground,
   optional

1 cup milk

Dissolve the yeast and sugar in ⅓ cup of the lukewarm water. Let stand 5–10 minutes. Mix the flour, salt, and mahlab in a large bowl, making a depression in the center. Pour the milk, remaining water, and dissolved yeast into the center of the flour. Begin mixing the flour with the liquid until all the flour is well worked into the dough.

Knead until a smooth dough results and the sides of the bowl are clean. (Occasionally dip your hands in more water while kneading to give a smooth, elastic finish.)

Cover the dough with a towel and let it rise in a warm place until it doubles in volume (1–2 hours). Divide into 6 equal parts and form into smooth balls. Cover the dough balls and let rise again on a cloth, about 30 minutes. Roll the balls into ¼- to ½-inch thick circles. After rolling all the balls, press them firmly in the center with a special mold for holy bread, or if you don't have the mold, leave plain. Using a toothpick, prick holes of the 3 points of a triangle just outside the last ring of the mold, spacing the triangles in four equal places around the design. (Be sure the holes do not touch the ring.) Cover the dough and let rise 35–40 minutes.

Bake at 400°F for 15–20 minutes or until golden brown.

NOTE: When removing the bread from the oven, you could wipe both sides of the loaf with a cloth dipped in rose water. In the Antioch Orthodox religion, 5 loaves are offered to the church. The seal taken from the first loaf becomes Holy Communion; the second, for the Mother of God; the third, for the angels and saints; the fourth, for the living; and the fifth, for the deceased. Mahlab is available in Middle Eastern specialty grocery stores.

Soups

Soup is a popular dish in Lebanon that is made from a variety of cereals and vegetables. A favorite winter soup is made from *kishk*, which is yogurt and burghul fermented together, dried, and ground. Most Arabic soups are hearty dishes and may be used as the main course.

In Lebanon, *kishk* is made by individual families once a year during the summer. The yogurt and burghul are put in the sun to dry. A favorite place is rooftops that are flat and clean. When it is time to grind the dried yogurt and burghul into *kishk*, relatives will help each other in completing this project. This is a time for mixing merriment with work!

NOTES

- *Zafra* are the foamy curds resulting from the boiling of meat in water. Remove by skimming as they form.

- A cinnamon stick is always added to the water for extra flavoring.

- When using parsley, add during the last 5 minutes to retain its flavor and color.

- *Kishk* is available in Middle Eastern specialty grocery stores.

Kishk Soup

Shurbat al-Kishk

MAKES 8 SERVINGS

½ **pound lamb, finely diced**

1 small potato, peeled and finely chopped, optional

1 large onion, coarsely chopped

3–4 large cloves garlic, coarsely chopped

1 cup kishk

4–5 cups water

⅛ **teaspoon pepper**

Salt to taste

Sauté the lamb and potato in a saucepan for a few minutes. Add the onions and garlic and continue sautéing. Add the kishk and continue sautéing for a few minutes. Stir constantly after the kishk has been added to prevent lumping and scorching.

Gradually add the water until a smooth mixture is formed. Cook for about 20 minutes or until thickened (consistency of cream gravy), stirring occasionally.

NOTE: Kishk is typically salty, so adjust accordingly. The meat may be omitted if desired. Kishk is often served during the winter months.

Meatball Soup

Shurbat al-Qima

MAKES 8 SERVINGS

1 small onion, minced

½ pound ground beef or lamb

½ cup parsley, finely chopped

6–8 cups cold water

1 cinnamon stick

½ cup uncooked rice

1 ripe tomato, diced, optional

Butter for sautéing

Salt and pepper to taste

Powdered cinnamon to serve

Mix the onions with the salt and pepper. Add the meat and a few leaves of chopped parsley. Mix well. Make meatballs (kafta) the size of a walnut. Brown the meatballs in the butter.

Add a small amount of water (½ cup) to the skillet to deglaze the residue. Empty the meatballs and the stock into a saucepan and add the cinnamon stick and the remaining water. Let it boil on medium heat for 10 minutes, then add the rice, tomatoes, and additional salt to taste. Cook for about 30 minutes or until the rice is tender.

Add the remaining chopped parsley during the last 5 minutes of cooking time. Serve the soup with a dash of cinnamon on top.

NOTE: Parsley should not be overcooked in soup.

Meat Soup with Kibbi Balls

Shurbat al-Mawzat ma' Kibbi

MAKES 8 SERVINGS

2–3 lamb or 1–2 beef shanks

1 small onion, chopped

⅛ teaspoon cinnamon

7–8 cups cold water

¼ cup uncooked rice

½ Basic Kibbi recipe (page 118)

Salt and pepper to taste

Place the meat shanks, onions, seasonings, and cold water in a pot. Cover and cook until a fork can pierce the meat, approximately 1 hour. Add the rice and continue cooking until done, about 30 minutes more.

In the meantime, take the kibbi and form it into about 3 dozen walnut-sized balls. These balls may be fried, baked, or broiled until just short of being done. When the shank meat is done, debone it, and return the meat to the broth with the rice. Add the kibbi balls and continue simmering for 15 minutes. Add more water as needed.

Shank Soup

Shurbat al-Mawzat

MAKES 8 SERVINGS

3–4 lamb or 2–3 beef shanks

1 cinnamon stick

½ cup uncooked long grain rice

2 tomatoes, diced

⅔ cup parsley, coarsely chopped

Salt and pepper to taste

Powdered cinnamon to serve

Place the lamb or beef shanks and the cinnamon stick in a large Dutch oven and completely cover with cold water. Cover and cook until a fork can pierce the meat, approximately 1 hour.

Remove the zafra (fat curds) during the cooking process. Add the rice, tomatoes, and salt and cook until the rice is tender.

In the last 5 minutes, add the parsley. To serve, sprinkle with a dash of cinnamon.

Tomato Soup

Shurbat al-Banadura

MAKES 8 SERVINGS

1–2 beef or lamb
   shanks
1 cinnamon stick
4 cups water
½ cup uncooked long
   grain rice
1 pound well-ripened
   tomatoes, squeezed
   and strained
Salt and pepper
   to taste

Place the shanks and cinnamon stick in a large Dutch oven with water. Add more water if needed to barely cover the shanks. Cover and cook until tender, about 1 hour.

Remove the zafra (fat curds) as they accumulate. Add the rice and cook for 20 minutes. Add the tomatoes, salt, and pepper. Simmer for 15–20 minutes.

Kibbi Soup

Shurbat al-Kibbi

MAKES 8 SERVINGS

½ **Basic Kibbi recipe**
¼ **cup pine nuts**
1 **teaspoon butter**
1 **onion, minced**
7–8 **cups water**
1 **cinnamon stick**
½ **cup uncooked long grain rice**
½ **cup parsley, coarsely chopped**
Salt and pepper to taste

Form the kibbi into walnut-sized balls. Make a hole in the center of each ball, place a few pine nuts inside and close. Brown the kibbi balls in the butter. Remove and set aside.

Sauté onions lightly. Add a small amount of water to the butter drippings. Pour the drippings into a large pan; add the remaining water, seasonings, and rice. Cook for 20 minutes.

Add the kibbi balls and simmer for 20 minutes or until the kibbi and rice are done. In the last 5 minutes, add the chopped parsley.

Vegetable Soup

Shurbat al-Khudar

MAKES 8 SERVINGS

1–2 beef or lamb shanks

6–8 cups water

1 cinnamon stick

1 stalk celery

2 carrots

1 small onion

1 parsnip

1 turnip

4–5 fresh string beans

2 medium tomatoes

1 medium potato

3–4 stems of parsley, chopped

Salt and pepper to taste

Cinnamon to taste

Place the shanks and cinnamon stick in a pan with the water. Cover and cook until tender, about 1 hour. Remove the zafra (fat curds) as they accumulate.

Dice all the vegetables, except the parsley, in 1-inch cubes and add with the seasonings to the shanks.

Cook until the vegetables are tender, about 20 minutes. Add the chopped parsley in the last 5 minutes of cooking. The soup is served with a dash of cinnamon.

Lentil Soup with Oil

Shurbat al-'Adas biz-Zayt

MAKES 8 SERVINGS

**1 cup split or whole
  dried lentils**
7–8 cups water
¼ cup uncooked rice
**1 large onion, coarsely
  chopped**
½ cup olive oil
**Salt and pepper
  to taste**

Rinse and drain the lentils. Place them in a pot with the water. Cook for 15 minutes. Add the rice.

Sauté the onions in the oil. Add salt and pepper. Add the onion mixture to the lentils and rice shortly after adding the rice. Cook for 20 minutes or until tender.

VARIATIONS

• There are two good variations of this recipe. Shurbat al-'Adas ma' Lahmi (Lentil Soup with Meat), which you prepare by adding a cup of chopped lamb to the onions, or Shurbat al-'Adas bis-Samni (Buttered Lentil Soup), which is prepared with butter instead of oil for sautéing the onions.

Lentils with Dried Beans and Rice

Makhlouta

MAKES 6 SERVINGS

¼ cup dried lentils

¼ cup dried
   garbanzo beans

¼ cup dried
   lima beans

¼ cup dried
   black beans

7–8 cups water

1 tablespoon cumin

1 large onion, coarsely
   chopped

½ cup olive oil

¼ cup rice

Salt to taste

Wash the dried beans and soak them overnight. Drain. Place the beans in a pot with the water and cover. Bring to a boil, add the cumin, reduce the heat, and cook on medium heat.

Meanwhile, sauté the onion in the oil. After the beans have cooked on medium heat for 30 minutes, add the rice, onions, and salt. Cook until all of the ingredients are tender, about 20 minutes more.

NOTE: The consistency of this soup is similar to chili; however, it may be thinned according to personal taste.

Lentils with Arabic Style Noodles
Rishta

MAKES 4–6 SERVINGS

1 ball unbaked Arabic
    Bread dough
1 cup dried lentils
7–8 cups water
1 large onion, coarsely
    chopped
1 tablespoon olive oil
1 clove garlic
1 tablespoon
    sweet basil
1 tablespoon
    coriander seed
4 cups Swiss chard,
    coarsely chopped
Salt and pepper
    to taste
Lemon wedges

Roll the bread dough like a piecrust and cut it into ¼-inch strips. Then slice the dough diagonally into ¼- to 1-inch-length pieces.

Rinse the lentils. Place the lentils and the water in a pot. Cook 30–45 minutes until almost tender. Sauté the onions in the oil. Mash together the garlic, basil, coriander, salt, and pepper. Add this mixture to the onions and continue sautéing until the onions are limp.

Add this mixture, the Swiss chard, and the bread dough pieces to the lentils. Cook until the Swiss chard and bread dough are tender, about 15 minutes. Serve with lemon wedges.

Lentils with Swiss Chard

‘Adas ‘bis-Silq

MAKES 8 SERVINGS

1 cup dried lentils

6 cups water

1 large potato, diced

½ bunch of Swiss
   chard, coarsely
   chopped

1 medium onion,
   coarsely chopped

3 tablespoons olive oil

Salt and pepper
   to taste

Lemon wedges

Wash the lentils. Put the lentils and the water in a pot, cover and cook until almost tender, about 30–45 minutes.

Add the potatoes; boil for 10 minutes. Add the Swiss chard. Meanwhile, sauté the onions with salt and pepper in the oil until the onions are golden brown.

Add the onions to the lentil mixture and cook until all of the vegetables are done, no more than 10 minutes. Serve with lemon wedges.

Salads

In the Middle East, most homes have a plentiful variety of vegetables in their gardens. In many parts of the United States there is also a wide selection, including some that are considered weeds—such as purslane and dandelions.

The basic dressing for all salads is olive oil, lemon juice, and garlic. Olive oil is used in the Middle East, primarily because it is so plentiful. Tartness is adjusted according to individual tastes.

Arabic Salad Supreme

Tabbouleh

MAKES 6 SERVINGS

¾ cup burghul
   (bulgur wheat, #2
   medium grind)
2 large bunches
   of parsley,
   approximately
   4 cups when finely
   chopped
1 cup finely chopped
   fresh mint or ¼–⅓
   cups dried mint
½ bunch of green
   onions, with green
   ends, finely chopped
⅛ teaspoon cinnamon
2–3 teaspoons
   kosher salt
1 small onion, finely
   chopped
1 or 2 large tomatoes,
   finely chopped
½–⅔ cup fresh
   lemon juice
½ cup olive oil
Pepper to taste
Fresh grape leaves,
   Romaine, or leaf
   lettuce

Rinse the burghul, drain, then squeeze the excess water out. Place the burghul in a large mixing bowl. Place the parsley, mint, and green onions in layers on top of the burghul in the order given. Add the seasonings to the onions and mix thoroughly.

Put onions on half of the top layer and tomatoes on the other half. Add lemon juice and toss the salad with a spoon and fork.

Just before serving, add the oil and toss thoroughly. Adjust seasoning to taste. Serve with grape leaves or lettuce on the side.

NOTE: Tabbouleh is typically eaten by hand. Use the grape leaves, Romaine lettuce, or head lettuce to pick up the salad in bite-size servings. Tabbouleh may be prepared 1–2 hours ahead of time by omitting the tomatoes and oil. Just cover with plastic wrap and refrigerate. Add the tomatoes and oil just before serving.

Tomato Salad

Slatat al-Banadura

MAKES 6 SERVINGS

1 small clove garlic
¼ teaspoon salt
¼ cup lemon juice
2 cucumbers
3 tomatoes
1 small onion,
  chopped
¼ cup olive oil

Mash the garlic and salt in a bowl. Add the lemon juice and mix well.

Cut the cucumbers and tomatoes into bite-size pieces. Add both to the garlic mixture along with the onions and oil. Mix gently. Adjust seasoning to taste.

NOTE: This is especially good with sides of hot peppers, olives, and Arabic Bread.

Lebanese Bread Salad

Makhlouta

MAKES 6 SERVINGS

½ loaf of Arabic bread

1 small clove garlic

½ cup lemon juice

½ cup parsley

3 green onions

1 small onion, finely chopped

1 cup fresh mint or ¼ cup dried mint

4–5 large leaves of Romaine lettuce, or ¼ head of lettuce

1 cucumber, peeled, quartered, and cut into small pieces

2–3 medium tomatoes, cut into 1-inch cubes

1 small hot pepper, minced, optional

½ teaspoon sumac, if available

½ cup olive oil

Salt and pepper to taste

Toast the bread to a golden brown and break into 1½-inch pieces. Set aside.

In a salad bowl, mash the garlic, or use a garlic press, and mix the garlic well with the salt and pepper. Add the lemon juice to the garlic mixture and blend well. Coarsely chop the parsley, green onions, and mint. Tear the lettuce as for a tossed green salad. Add the parsley, green onions, mint, cucumber, tomatoes, hot pepper, sumac, and toasted bread to the lemon and garlic mixture and toss thoroughly.

Just before serving, add the oil and toss well. Adjust seasoning to taste.

NOTE: Sumac is available in Middle Eastern specialty grocery stores or online.

Vegetable Salad

Slatat al-Khudar

MAKES 4 SERVINGS

1 clove garlic

¼ teaspoon kosher salt

½ small hot pepper, optional

¼ cup lemon juice

1 small onion, finely chopped

2 green onions, coarsely chopped

1 small green pepper

4 leaves Romaine lettuce, or other lettuce

1 medium cucumber

2 medium tomatoes

¼ cup olive oil

Several stems of parsley, coarsely chopped

Several stems of mint, coarsely chopped

Mash the garlic, salt, and hot pepper together. Add the lemon juice and mix well. Combine the parsley, mint, onion, and green onion. Set aside.

Cut all of the vegetables into chunks and add them to the garlic mixture. Add the parsley mixture and oil to the vegetables and garlic. Toss thoroughly. Adjust seasoning to taste.

NOTE: Any combination of vegetables may be used, depending upon what is available.

Purslane Salad
Slatat al-Farfhin (or Baqli)

MAKES 4 SERVINGS

4 bunches of purslane
1 clove garlic
½ teaspoon salt
¼ cup lemon juice
1 onion, chopped
¼ cup olive oil
1 tomato, chopped
1 cucumber, chopped

Pick or remove the tender green leaves and clusters at the end of the purslane stems. Discard the seed in the center of the clusters. Wash and drain.

Mash the garlic and salt together. Add the lemon juice and mix well. Add the purslane, onion, and olive oil. Add the tomato and cucumber. Adjust seasoning to taste. Toss lightly.

NOTE: Purslane is not typically available in grocery stores. It grows wild in yards and other places, especially around tomato or rose plants. It is considered a weed but makes an unusual and delicious salad. Pick it in the early morning or late afternoon, so the leaves will be crisp.

Green Beans with Potato Salad

Batata Mtabbli Ma' Lubyi

MAKES 4 SERVINGS

½ pound green beans
3 medium potatoes
1 small clove garlic
½ teaspoon salt
⅓ cup lemon juice
1 small onion, chopped
⅓ cup olive oil

Wash the green beans, then snip the ends and cut into 2-inch pieces. Cook the beans in salted water until tender but crisp, approximately 3–5 minutes. Drain and cool.

Boil the potatoes. Cool and cut into 1-inch cubes. Mash the garlic and salt together. Add the lemon juice and mix well. Add the potatoes, beans, onions, and oil. Toss well. Adjust seasoning to taste.

NOTE: This recipe may be prepared ahead of time for a thorough blending of flavors.

Green Bean Salad

Lubyi Mtabbli

MAKES 4–6 SERVINGS

1½ pounds
  green beans
1 small clove garlic
½ teaspoon kosher salt
⅓ cup lemon juice
1 small onion,
  chopped
2–3 stems parsley,
  coarsely chopped
⅓ cup olive oil

Wash the green beans, then snip the ends and cut into 2-inch pieces. Cook in salted water until tender but crisp, approximately 3–5 minutes. Drain and cool.

Mash the garlic and salt together. Add the lemon juice and mix well. Add the remaining ingredients and toss. Adjust seasoning to taste.

Cauliflower with Taratur
Qarnabit bit-Tahini

MAKES 4 SERVINGS

1 small head
  cauliflower,
  approximately
  1 pound
1 clove garlic
½ teaspoon kosher salt
3 tablespoons tahini
2 tablespoons water or
  cauliflower liquid
⅓ cup lemon juice

Rinse the cauliflower and break it into separate florets. Steam or cook in water for 10–15 minutes on a medium flame. When done, the cauliflower should be tender but firm.

Mash the garlic and salt in a bowl. Add the tahini and blend well, then add the water and mix thoroughly. Add the lemon juice and blend until the sauce is whitish and smooth.

Drain the cauliflower and place it in a shallow bowl. Carefully pour the tahini sauce over all of the cauliflower pieces—*do not stir.* Adjust seasoning to taste. Serve hot or cold.

Lebanese Potato Salad

Batata Mtabbli

MAKES 4–6 SERVINGS

4 large potatoes
1 small clove garlic
½ teaspoon kosher salt
½ teaspoon pepper
⅓ cup lemon juice
1 small onion,
   chopped
⅓–½ cup coarsely
   chopped parsley
⅓ cup olive oil

Boil the potatoes until tender but firm. Cool, peel and cut into 1-inch cubes. Mash the garlic with the seasonings.

Add the lemon juice and stir well. Add the rest of the ingredients and toss, mixing well. Adjust seasoning to taste.

Lima Bean Salad

Fasulya biz-Zayt

MAKES 4–6 SERVINGS

1 cup dried white
    lima beans
1 clove garlic
½ teaspoon kosher salt
¼ cup lemon juice
¼ cup olive oil
½ cup finely chopped
    parsley
3 scallions, chopped,
    optional

Wash the beans thoroughly and soak them in water overnight. Drain the beans, then place them in a saucepan and cover with fresh water. Cook until tender but firm, about 1–1½ hours. (Check occasionally and add water to cover if needed. The cooking time will depend on the age of the dried beans.) Drain the beans, reserving ½ cup of liquid.

In a bowl, mash the garlic and salt together. Add the lemon juice and mix well. Add the reserved bean liquid and olive oil to the lemon juice mixture. Add the beans. Toss gently. Adjust seasoning to taste.

Garnish with parsley and scallions, which are sprinkled in a ring on top and in the center. Serve hot or cold, as a salad or a side dish.

Potatoes with Taratur Sauce

Batat bit-Tahini

MAKES 4 SERVINGS

4 medium potatoes
1 small clove garlic
½ teaspoon kosher salt
4 tablespoons tahini
2 tablespoons water
⅓ cup lemon juice
4 stems parsley, finely
  chopped

Boil the potatoes until tender but firm, about 15 minutes. Peel and cut into ½-inch cubes and place in a bowl.

Mash the garlic and salt together in a small bowl. Add the tahini and blend well. Add the water and mix thoroughly. Add the lemon juice and blend until the sauce is a creamy white. Mix in the parsley.

Pour the tahini mixture over the potatoes and mix gently so as not to mash the potatoes. Adjust seasoning to taste. This may be served warm or cold.

NOTE: This is especially good with baked or fried fish.

Black-Eyed Pea Salad

Lubyi Msallat

MAKES 4–6 SERVINGS

1 cup dried black-
  eyed peas
1 clove garlic
½ teaspoon kosher salt
¼ cup lemon juice
1 small onion, finely
  chopped
½ cup parsley,
  chopped
¼ cup olive oil

Wash the beans well and soak them in water overnight. Drain and place in a saucepan with water to cover. Cook on a medium flame until tender but firm. (Check occasionally and add water to cover if needed. The cooking time will depend on the age of the dried beans.)

Mash the garlic and salt together in a large bowl. Add the lemon juice and onions. Drain the beans, reserving 1 cup of liquid. Add the liquid to the lemon juice mixture. Add the drained beans. Mix well, being careful not to mash the beans.

Garnish with chopped parsley in a ring in the center. Pour oil on top. Adjust seasoning to taste. Serve hot or cold.

NOTE: Two 8-ounce packages of frozen black-eyed peas may be used. Follow the directions on the package and proceed as above.

Eggplant Salad

Batinjan Mtabbal

MAKES 4–6 SERVINGS

1 large eggplant
1 small clove garlic
½ teaspoon kosher salt
⅓ cup lemon juice
1 tablespoon olive oil
4 stems parsley, finely
   chopped

Place the eggplant on a baking sheet and bake at 350°F until tender but firm. Peel and slice in large pieces (about 2-inch pieces). Place the eggplant in a large bowl.

Mash the garlic and salt together. Add the lemon juice and blend well. Stir in the oil and pour the mixture over the top of the eggplant. Adjust seasoning to taste. Garnish with parsley. Serve warm or cold.

NOTE: The eggplant may be cubed instead of sliced and tossed with a few chopped pieces of parsley.

Brain Appetizer

Nkha' at Mtabbli

MAKES 4 SERVINGS

1 pound lamb or beef brains

1 teaspoon kosher salt, plus ½ teaspoon

1 clove garlic

2 teaspoons pepper

¼ cup olive oil

½ cup chopped parsley

Juice of one lemon, adjust to desired tartness

Rinse the brains and place them in a pan of water to cover. Add one teaspoon of the salt. Cook for 10–15 minutes on medium flame or until tender and the fork pierces the meat easily. Remove the brains and peel off the skin and blood vessels. Cool. Cut the brains in bite-size pieces and place in a shallow bowl.

Meanwhile, mash the garlic, remaining ½ teaspoon of salt, and pepper together. Add the lemon juice and oil and mix well. Pour the mixture over the brains, covering all pieces. Adjust seasoning to taste. Sprinkle the parsley on top. Do not stir.

Lamb Tongue Salad

Lsanat Mtabbli

6 lamb tongues

1 clove garlic

2 teaspoons kosher salt, plus ½ teaspoon

⅓ cup lemon juice

¼ cup olive oil

Pepper to taste

Chopped parsley for garnish

Rinse the lamb tongues well and place them in a pan. Cover with water and add 2 teaspoons of salt. Cook until well done and the fork pierces the meat easily. Remove the tongues, cool slightly, and peel off the skin. Cut into 1-inch squares.

Mash the garlic, remaining salt, and pepper together. Add the lemon juice and olive oil, and blend well. Add the tongue pieces to the lemon mixture. Toss and adjust seasoning to taste. Garnish with parsley.

NOTE: This is good as a main course or an appetizer. Another version is to pour Parsley in Tahini Sauce (page 3) over the tongue.

Fish

One favorite fish in Lebanon is called bizri, a small, thin fish that is deep-fried and eaten like French fries. Other favorites are called hanklis and Sultan Ibrahim and are not generally found in North America. However, ling cod, kingfish, bass, and perch can be substituted. After frying fish, one custom is to fry pieces of Arabic bread in the fish residue to be served as an accompaniment.

Herring Hors D'Oeuvres

Sanamura

MAKES 4–6 SERVINGS

1–2 smoked herring
2 cloves garlic
¼ cup olive oil
½ cup parsley, finely
   chopped
½ cup lemon juice

Debone and cut the herring into small pieces. Cut the garlic in small pieces. Mix the herring, garlic, and remaining ingredients.

NOTE: Serve with Arabic Bread (page 13).

Grilled Fish

Samak Mishwi

MAKES 6 SERVINGS

2 pounds perch, ling
   cod, or king fish
1 Tahini Sauce recipe
   (page 3)
Salt
Olive oil

Wash the fish; season with salt and let stand for an hour. Thoroughly rub the fish with olive oil. Grill on a charcoal grill, 15 minutes per side, and serve with tahini sauce.

Snails

Bizzaq

2 dozen fresh snails
1 tablespoon kosher
    salt, plus 1 teaspoon
1 clove garlic
½ cup olive oil
Juice of one lemon
Salt and pepper
    to taste

Rinse the snails well and boil for 20 minutes. Remove from the flame, and discard water. Add fresh hot water and a tablespoon of salt and boil for 15 more minutes.

While the snails are boiling, prepare the sauce. Mash the garlic and remaining salt together. Add the lemon juice and oil and mix well. Adjust seasoning to taste with salt and pepper.

Remove the snails from their shells and dip in sauce.

NOTE: This is a great appetizer. Dormant snails can be bought. Soak them in cold water until they become active.

Fish with Pine Nut Sauce

Samak Ma'at-Taratur

MAKES 6–8 SERVINGS

3–5 pounds perch, halibut, or cod
Olive oil
Salt

SAUCE

1½ cup pine nuts
2–3 large cloves garlic
1–1½ cups lemon juice
Salt to taste
Chopped parsley to garnish

Rub the fish with olive oil. Wrap in heavy parchment paper that has been well oiled. Bake for 30 minutes at 425°F or until the fish flakes easily with a fork.

Meanwhile prepare the sauce. In a food processor, grind together the pine nuts, garlic, and salt until the nuts are of a dough-like consistency. Gradually add the lemon juice, mixing constantly until it is the consistency of yogurt.

Remove the paper from the baked fish and place the fish on a serving platter. Pour the sauce over the fish. Garnish with parsley around the edge of the fish.

Fish with Rice

Sayyadiyyi

MAKES 6–8 SERVINGS

3 pounds whole ling cod, king fish, or perch

1 cup olive oil

2 cups water

2 large onions, coarsely chopped

2 cups uncooked rice, long grain

1 tablespoon cumin

2 lemons, cut into wedges

Kosher salt

Salt and pepper to taste

Wash the fish, salt inside and out. Let stand for 1 hour. Fry the fish in the olive oil for 3–4 minutes per side. Set on a platter. Remove the head from the fried fish and boil it in the water on a medium flame for about 30 minutes. Strain the liquid.

Brown the onions until golden brown in the fish residue, adding more olive oil if needed. Add the rice, cumin, and salt and pepper. Sauté the rice with the onions for a few minutes. Add the strained liquid plus water to measure 4 cups. Cover and cook over medium heat for 20 minutes, then simmer 10 additional minutes or until the rice is done.

Place the rice on a platter. Debone the fish and spread over the rice. Add salt and pepper to taste. Garnish with lemon wedges.

Marinated Fish Fillets

Filetto as-Samak

MAKES 4–6 SERVINGS

2 pounds sliced white fish fillets

1 cup olive oil

⅔ cup vinegar

1 tablespoon butter

1 teaspoon sage

1 egg

1 tablespoon finely chopped parsley

1 cup breadcrumbs

1 tomato, sliced, optional

1 lemon, cut into wedges, optional

Salt and pepper to taste

Cover the fillets with the olive oil and vinegar (the fish should be completely covered so adjust the amount of oil and vinegar as needed). Refrigerate and marinate for 2 hours.

Drain and place in a well-buttered baking pan. Sprinkle salt, pepper, and sage over the fish. Beat the egg well, add the parsley and pour the mixture over the top of the fish. Sprinkle breadcrumbs over the entire surface.

Bake at 450°F for 10–15 minutes or until the fish flakes easily with a fork. Serve with tomato slices or sliced lemons.

Baked Fish Supreme

Tajin

MAKES 6 SERVINGS

1 large whole fish
(3–4 pounds)
Salt
Oil

SAUCE

3 large onions,
  julienned
1½ cup olive oil
2 teaspoons pepper
2 cups tahini
½ cup water
1½ cup lemon juice
Salt

Clean and scale the fish (or buy cleaned and scaled). Salt inside and out. Let it stand for one hour. Grease the baking dish and the fish with oil (not necessarily olive oil).

Bake the fish at 400°F for 25–30 minutes or until done and the fish will easily flake with a fork.

While the fish is baking, prepare the sauce. Sauté the onions in olive oil until golden brown. Add the salt and pepper. Mix the tahini and water thoroughly, until they thicken slightly. Gradually add the lemon juice, mixing until it becomes fluffy and thick like gravy. Add the tahini to the onions and cook over medium flame, bringing to a boil. Boil for about 10 minutes.

Pour the sauce over the whole fish and bake 10 minutes more at 350°F. Serve hot.

NOTE: This is best served with rice.

Baked Fish with Tahini Sauce

Samak bit-Taratur

MAKES 6–8 SERVINGS

**1 large whole fish
(3–5 pounds)
Kosher salt
Oil**

**SAUCE
1 clove garlic
1 cup tahini
¼ cup water
⅔ cup lemon juice
¼ cup parsley, finely
  chopped, plus more
  for serving
Salt to taste**

Wash the fish, salt the inside and out. Let stand for one hour. Grease a baking dish and the fish with oil. Bake at 400°F for 25–30 minutes or until done and the fish flakes easily with a fork.

Prepare the sauce while the fish is baking. Mash the garlic and salt together. Add the tahini and mix well with a fork. Add the water and mix well. Add the lemon juice and continue mixing until it becomes thick like gravy. More water may be added if needed. Add the chopped parsley.

Remove the fish from the oven and place on a platter. Cool. Pour the sauce over the fish and garnish with parsley leaves.

NOTE: If the sauce is placed over hot fish, the oil in the tahini will separate. The fish may be deboned and served separately on a platter. The sauce is then served in a bowl with the chopped parsley on top.

Savory Salmon with Spinach

Samak bis-Sbanikh

MAKES 4–6 SERVINGS

2–3 pounds whole salmon

6 stalks of celery

2 bunches of fresh spinach

1 bunch of green onions

1 bunch of parsley

½ cup olive oil

¾ cup water

⅔ cup fresh lemon juice

Sage, fresh or dried

Salt and pepper to taste

Clean the fish and rub a little sage inside the cavity. Place the fish in a roasting pan. Clean all the vegetables. Cut the celery in half lengthwise and then in ½-inch pieces.

Cover the fish with the celery. Cut the spinach in 2-inch lengths and place it on top of the celery. Dice the onions and coarsely chop the parsley. Place in that order on top of the celery. Season to taste.

Pour the olive oil and water over the fish. Bake at 425°F for 30 minutes. Remove the pan from the oven, stir the vegetables gently, add the lemon juice and bake for an additional 10 minutes. Serve the fish on a platter surrounded by the vegetables.

NOTE: The broth may be served separately.

Entrées

A country's diet generally consists of what is raised and grown on its terrain and that which is found in its waters. Hence the diet of the Middle East—with the Mediterranean, its rivers, and its temperate climate—consists primarily of lamb or mutton, seafood, grains, fresh vegetables, and a variety of fruits. Goat and beef products are also plentiful. A popular meat dish is *kafta* which is made with ground beef or lamb, minced onions, chopped parsley, and seasoned with cinnamon or other middle eastern spices. The base *kafta* recipe is used in several applications, whether made into patties or kabobs and grilled or incorporated into stews or casseroles. Grilled *kafta* is widely enjoyed in the middle east and is often the center of a barbeque feast.

The entrees in this section are not the only meat entrees in this book. There are many more to try in the chapters on Mihshi, Kibbi, Fish, yogurt, and Vegetarian dishes.

Basic Hamburger à la The Middle East
Kafta

MAKES 4 SERVINGS

1 pound finely ground lean beef or lamb
1 small onion, minced
½ cup finely chopped parsley
1 teaspoon kosher salt
¼ teaspoon pepper
¼ teaspoon cinnamon
⅛ teaspoon allspice

Mix ingredients well. Shape into hamburger-size patties. Broil or grill.

NOTE: This is a basic recipe to be used in a number of the recipes that follow.

Kafta with Peas

Kafta Ma' Bazilla

MAKES 4 SERVINGS

1 pound finely ground
   lean beef or lamb
1 small onion, minced
1 teaspoon salt
¼ teaspoon pepper
¼ teaspoon cinnamon
⅛ teaspoon allspice
1 tablespoon butter
2 (8-ounce) packages
   of frozen peas
1 (8-ounce) can of
   tomato sauce
1 cup water
Rice for serving

Mix the lamb, onion, salt, pepper, cinnamon, and allspice well. Form the mixture into 1-inch patties. Sauté in butter. Add the frozen peas, tomato sauce, and water.

Bring to boil, lower the heat and continue cooking until the peas are tender. Serve over rice.

Grilled Kafta

Kafta Mishwiyyi

MAKES 4 SERVINGS

1 pound finely ground lean beef or lamb

1 small onion, minced

½ cup finely chopped parsley

1 teaspoon salt

¼ teaspoon pepper

¼ teaspoon cinnamon

Mix all of the ingredients well. Form the meat into individual long, cylinder shapes around a skewer. Broil in the oven or grill over charcoal.

NOTE: Serve with Arabic bread and yogurt.

Baked Kafta

Kafta bis-Sayniyyi

MAKES 6–8 SERVINGS

1 pound finely ground
   beef or lamb

1 small onion,
   chopped

1 egg

½ cup bread or
   cracker crumbs

1½ teaspoon salt

¼ teaspoon pepper

¼ teaspoon cinnamon

¼ teaspoon allspice

4 medium potatoes

1 (8-ounce) can of
   tomato sauce

3 cups water,
   approximately

Thoroughly mix all of the ingredients except the potatoes, tomato sauce, and water. Form the mixture into hamburger patties about 1-inch thick. Place them next to each other in the bottom of a 9 x 12-inch pan.

Peel and slice the potatoes to a thickness of ½ inch and place them over the meat. Mix the tomato sauce in about 3 cups of water and pour over the potatoes (potatoes are barely covered). Bake at 400°F for 45–60 minutes, or until potatoes are tender.

Grilled Meat Kabobs

Lahm Mishwi (Kabob)

MAKES 6–8 SERVINGS

2 pounds lean lamb
  or beef, cut in
  2-inch cubes

⅛ teaspoon cinnamon

1 large onion, cut in
  2-inch chunks

Salt and pepper
  to taste

Fresh mint

Sprinkle the meat with the seasonings. Skewer the meat and onions, alternating (3 to 1, or as desired) meat with onions.

Grill over charcoal until desired tenderness. When serving, garnish with fresh mint.

NOTE: Meat can be marinated in ⅓ cup olive oil for an hour before grilling. Kabobs are usually eaten medium rare.

Elegant Egg-Stuffed Meatloaf
Kafta Mihshi bil-Bayd

MAKES 6 SERVINGS

2 pounds ground lamb
    or beef
1 large onion, grated
¼ teaspoon cinnamon
¼ teaspoon allspice
½ cup soda crackers,
    finely ground, or
    breadcrumbs
1 egg, lightly beaten
1 cup parsley, finely
    chopped
6 hard-boiled eggs,
    peeled
1 tablespoon butter
Salt and pepper
    to taste

With your fingers work the onions and seasonings into the meat. Add the crackers and egg; mix thoroughly. Form the meat mixture into three loaves. Flatten the loaves until they're ½ to 1-inch thick. Sprinkle the tops of the loaves generously with parsley.

Place 2 hard-boiled eggs on top of the parsley. Roll as in a jelly roll, smoothing all sides.

Place the loaves in a buttered baking pan and bake at 375°F for 30 minutes or until brown.

NOTE: This is excellent for a buffet dinner or as an hors d'oeuvres.

Grilled Lamb Supreme

Shawarma

MAKES 4–6 SERVINGS

1 pound lamb shoulder
1 pound leg of lamb
Salt and pepper
  to taste

Slice the meat into 4–6-inch squares that are 1-inch thick. Alternate lean and fat pieces on the skewer of a rotisserie.

As soon as the outside is cooked (to individual taste), slice the meat very thin. Sprinkle with seasonings. Continue grilling and slicing as needed.

NOTE: This Grilled Lamb Supreme is delicious when sliced into a half loaf of Arabic bread. Add chopped lettuce, tomatoes, and onions. Top with tahini.

Meat Rolls Supreme

Sambusik bil-Lahm

MAKES 6–8 SERVINGS

FILLING

½ cup pine nuts

2 tablespoons butter

2 pounds leg of lamb, finely ground

2 medium onions, finely chopped

⅛ teaspoon cinnamon

½ cup lemon juice, optional

Salt and pepper to taste

FILO

1 pound filo dough

1 cup butter, melted

Sauté the pine nuts in 2 tablespoons of butter until golden brown. Remove the pine nuts from the butter and set aside. Sauté the meat and onions in the remainder of the butter until lightly browned. Stir in the seasonings and pine nuts. Cool. (If a tart flavor is desired, add lemon juice and mix ingredients well.)

Take 2 sheets of filo dough and brush the tops with the melted butter. Place the filling (in the thickness of a cigar) on the buttered side along the long edge to within 1-inch of both ends. Roll the dough one turn over the filling. Turn the 2 short ends of the dough toward center to secure the meat in the roll and continue rolling as for a jelly roll. Repeat for the second sheet of filo.

Arrange the rolls on a buttered baking pan, brush the tops lightly with butter and bake in a preheated oven at 400°F for 25–30 minutes or until the dough is lightly browned. Slice the rolls into the desired length before serving.

NOTE: Excellent for hors d'oeuvres.

Brain Omelet

Ijjit an-Nkha'at

MAKES 4 SERVINGS

1 pound lamb or beef
   brains
2 teaspoons salt, plus
   salt and pepper
   to taste
1 tablespoon
   lemon juice
4 eggs
½ cup parsley, finely
   chopped
1 small onion, finely
   chopped

Rinse the brains thoroughly. Place the brains, salt, lemon juice, and enough water to cover in a pan. Bring to a boil and cook until a fork pierces the meat easily. Drain and devein the brains and chop.

Beat the eggs and add the parsley. Add the onions after sprinkling them with the salt and pepper. Add the chopped brain and carefully mix. Place on a greased 7-inch pan that has been heated.

NOTE: Bake at 375°F for 15–20 minutes or until done, when the brains are firm to the touch.

Lemoned Lamb Liver

Mhamsa

MAKES 4 SERVINGS

1 pound lamb liver
2 medium onions,
  chopped
2 tablespoons olive oil
¼ cup lemon juice
Salt and pepper to
  taste

Cut the liver into 1-inch pieces. Sauté the onions in the oil until limp. Add the liver and seasonings and continue sautéing for a few minutes. Add the lemon juice and water to barely cover. Bring to a quick boil.

Lower the heat and simmer for about 5 minutes.

NOTE: This must be cooked rapidly with a maximum cooking time of 10 minutes.

Grilled Lamb Liver

Qasbi Mishwiyyi

MAKES 4 SERVINGS

1 pound lamb liver
2 onions
Salt and pepper to
    taste
Cherry tomatoes,
    optional

Cut the liver and onions into 2-inch chunks. Sprinkle with salt and pepper. Alternate liver, onions, and tomatoes on skewers.

Grill on charcoal for 5–7 minutes, or until done, turning constantly.

Arabic Sausage

Makanek

MAKES 4 SERVINGS

2 pounds lean lamb,
   coarsely ground

2 pounds pork,
   coarsely ground

2 cups sweet red wine

½ cup coriander seed

2 tablespoons allspice

1 tablespoon
   cinnamon

Salt and pepper
   to taste

Lamb or pork casing

Mix all of the stuffing ingredients thoroughly. Refrigerate for 3–4 hours, stirring occasionally. Stuff the filling into the casing, using a 1-inch funnel slipped into the casing as a guide to insert the sausage mixture. With thread, tie off the sausages at the desired length.

Age by hanging in a cold place or refrigerate for two days before freezing. To serve, cut into links and fry or grill.

NOTE: If casing is unavailable, refrigerate for 24 hours, then make into patties or rolls and freeze.

Preserved Lamb

Qawrama

MAKES 6 SERVINGS

1 pound lamb shoulder, finely ground
Salt and pepper to taste

Place the meat in a pot. Add salt (should be on the salty side) and pepper to taste. Cook on high heat for a few minutes. Lower the heat to medium and continue cooking, stirring occasionally.

When the fat is completely rendered, about 30–45 minutes, and the meat is light brown, the qawrama is ready. Pour the meat in a wide-mouth glass or earthenware jar. Cover and refrigerate. A fat layer will form on top.

NOTE: Use this in preparation for various other dishes. Scoop both the fat and the meat from the container and serve with fried eggs (kishk). Qawrama is also good when cooked with vegetables.

Peas with Lamb

Bazilla bil-Lahm

MAKES 4 SERVINGS

1 pound tender young
 peas and pods

1 pound ground beef
 or lamb

⅛ teaspoon cinnamon

1 large onion, chopped

2 cups water

2 tomatoes, finely
 chopped or
 1 (8-ounce) can
 tomato sauce

Salt and pepper
 to taste

Shell the peas and save the soft outside portion of the pea pod. This is done by bending the pod in half lengthwise, which will split the pod in half. From the split, peel off the soft portions.

Brown the meat with the seasonings. Add the onions and sauté until golden. Add the water and simmer for 15 minutes. Add the tomatoes or tomato sauce and cook for 10 minutes more. Add the peas and pods and let simmer for 15 minutes.

NOTE: Frozen peas may be substituted. Pods should be omitted. Adjust the cooking time per the package instructions.

Okra with Meat

Bamyi bil-Lahm

MAKES 4 SERVINGS

1 pound fresh
   tender okra
1 tablespoon olive oil
¾ pound ground beef
   or lamb
1 medium onion,
   chopped
2 cloves garlic,
   chopped
1 teaspoon ground
   coriander or
   2 teaspoons
   coriander seed
1 cup water
1 (8-ounce) can
   tomato sauce
½–¾ cup lemon juice
Salt and pepper
   to taste

Rinse the okra and cut off the stems. Dry. Sauté the okra in olive oil until lightly brown. (The okra may be brushed with butter or margarine and placed under the broiler to brown.) Set aside.

Sauté the meat in the leftover oil for about 5 minutes, stirring constantly. Add the onions, garlic, and seasonings and continue sautéing until the onions are limp. Add the water and simmer for 15 minutes. Then add the tomato sauce and lemon juice (add more lemon juice if you prefer a tart taste).

Add the okra and gently stir the mixture once. Do not stir it again. Cook for 10–15 minutes or until the okra is tender.

NOTE: Frozen okra may be substituted. Omit the sautéing if using frozen.

Green Beans with Meat

Lubyi bil-Lahm

MAKES 4 SERVINGS

2 pounds fresh
  green beans
1 pound lamb shoulder
2 medium onions,
  chopped
2 cloves garlic,
  chopped
⅛ teaspoon cinnamon
¼ cup water
1 (8-ounce) can
  tomato sauce or
  3 medium-sized
  fresh tomatoes,
  finely chopped
Salt and pepper
  to taste

Clean, stem, and cut the beans in about 2-inch lengths and set aside.

Cut the meat into 1-inch cubes and sauté for 10 minutes. Add the onions, garlic, and seasonings; sauté for 5 minutes more. Add the water and simmer for 10 minutes. Add the beans and tomatoes, toss. Add water to half the depth of the meat and bean mixture.

Cover and cook for 20–25 minutes on a medium flame or until the beans and meat are tender. Stir occasionally.

NOTE: Frozen green beans may be substituted.

Lamb-Asparagus Casserole

Halyun bil-Lahm

MAKES 4 SERVINGS

1 pound fresh
  asparagus
½ pound lamb
  shoulder, coarsely
  chopped
1 clove garlic,
  chopped, optional
1 medium onion,
  chopped
⅛ teaspoon cinnamon
⅛ teaspoon allspice
2 tablespoons butter
1 cup water
Salt and pepper
  to taste

Cut tender asparagus into 2-inch lengths. Rinse, drain, and set aside.

Sauté the meat, garlic, onions, and seasonings in butter. Add the asparagus and simmer for 5 minutes. Add the water and cook for about 20–25 minutes or until the tender.

NOTE: This can also be cooked in a covered casserole and baked for 15–20 minutes at 400°F. Serve with rice.

Lima Bean and Lamb Stew

Fasulya bil-Lahm

MAKES 4 SERVINGS

1½ pounds lamb
  shoulder, cubed in
  small chunks

1 cup dry lima beans,
  soaked overnight or
  2 packages frozen
  lima beans

2 medium onions,
  finely diced

1 can whole tomatoes,
  or 3 medium-sized
  fresh tomatoes,
  chopped

⅛ teaspoon cinnamon

Olive oil

Salt and pepper
  to taste

Sauté cubed lamb in a little olive oil with seasonings until browned.

Add onions, continue sautéing until just limp. Add drained, soaked lima beans to meat and onions. Barely cover with water and cook beans and meat for 30 minutes. Add chopped tomatoes and continue cooking for another 20 minutes or until beans and meat are tender. (If frozen lima beans are used, total cooking time will be 25–30 minutes).

Add tomatoes the last 10 minutes.

NOTE: When using dried lima beans, additional water may be needed.

Stewed Eggplants

Mnazlit al-Batinjan

MAKES 4 SERVINGS

1 pound lamb, cubed
  in 1 inch pieces
1 large onion, chopped
⅛ teaspoon allspice
⅛ teaspoon allspice
½ cup water
1 medium-sized
  eggplant, peeled
  and cubed into 2–3
  inch pieces
1 can whole tomatoes,
  or 3 fresh tomatoes,
  chopped
Salt and pepper
  to taste

Sauté meat, onions and spices in a casserole. Add water, cover and let braise for 15 minutes.

Add eggplant, tomatoes and toss lightly. Cover and let simmer for 15–20 minutes. Eggplants should be firm but done.

NOTE: Serve with vermicelli rice.

Potato Stew

Yakhnit al-batata

MAKES 4 SERVINGS

1 pound lamb
   shoulder, cubed

⅛ teaspoon cinnamon

1 large onion, chopped

4 large potatoes,
   peeled and cut into
   small chunks

1 (8-ounce) can of
   tomato sauce

Salt and pepper
   to taste

Sauté the meat and seasonings slowly for a few minutes in a saucepan. Add the onions and potatoes. Toss with a closed lid. Slowly cook covered for 10 minutes on a low flame.

Add the tomato sauce and water to half the depth of the ingredients. Simmer until done, 20–30 minutes.

Meat with Whole Wheat

Harisa

MAKES 6 SERVINGS

2 pounds lamb shanks
1 stick cinnamon
2 cups whole wheat
   kernels
2 cups plain yogurt
Salt and pepper
   to taste

In a deep pan, completely cover the meat with cold water, add seasonings, bring to boil and remove the zafra (fat curd). Continue simmering until the meat is just tender. Rinse the whole wheat kernels, then add to the meat. Bring to a boil, reduce the heat to medium and stir constantly until it has the consistency of gravy.

Remove from the heat, debone the meat, and return it to the wheat mixture. Mix and serve with plain yogurt.

Lamb-Vegetable Stew

Yakhnit at Khudar bil-Lahm

MAKES 4 SERVINGS

2 stalks of celery

3 carrots

2 potatoes

2 turnips

1 parsnip

1 large onion

1 pound lamb, cut into
1½-inch cubes

2 cloves garlic, minced

⅛ teaspoon allspice

Salt and pepper
to taste

Cut all of the vegetables into 2-inch lengths. Place all of the ingredients in a pot and cover with water to 2 inches above the ingredients.

Cover and cook on a medium flame for 45–60 minutes, until the meat is tender, stirring occasionally. Add additional water if needed.

Eggs Fried with Chicken Giblets

Bayd Ma' Hwahis ad-Djaj

MAKES 1–2 SERVINGS

¼ **pound giblets (or giblets of one chicken)**

3 eggs

Oil or butter

Salt and pepper to taste

Cut the gizzards and heart into small chunks. Sauté in the oil or butter, then add the liver, sauté until tender. Add the eggs and seasonings to the giblets and cook like an omelet or leave the eggs whole on top of the giblets.

NOTE: In the Middle East, this is usually served for breakfast but is excellent for lunch or any other time.

Chicken with Vegetables Par Excellence

Mlukhiyyi

MAKES 4–6 SERVINGS

1 chicken, fryer, or
   4 lamb shanks

⅛ teaspoon cinnamon

2 large onions, finely
   chopped

1 cup vinegar with
   ¼ cup water

2 pounds mlukhiyyi,
   fresh or 1 pound dry

2 loaves Arabic bread
   toasted until golden
   brown

2 cups rice, cooked for
   serving

Salt and pepper
   to taste

Place the chicken and seasonings in a pot and cover with water. Cook until the chicken is tender, about 45 minutes. Remove the chicken and debone. Place in a serving dish and keep warm. Set the broth aside.

Meanwhile, cover the onions with the vinegar and water. Add a dash of salt and pepper. Soak for 45 minutes. If fresh mlukhiyyi is used, chop the leaves razor thin. Add mlukhiyyi in the chicken broth and cook for 15 minutes. Place in a soup tureen.

Break the toasted bread into 1-inch pieces. To serve, place a handful of bread in the bottom of each individual soup bowl or plate. Place a scoop of onions with a little juice over the bread; add the desired amount of rice and top with a scoop of the mlukhiyyi and chicken.

NOTE: Check your local market for mlukhiyyi, a green leafy vegetable. In the Middle East, it is available in the winter and early spring.

Baked Chicken

Djaj Mhammar

MAKES 4 SERVINGS

¼ **cup olive oil**
¼ **cup lemon juice**
1 **teaspoon salt**
1 **teaspoon oregano**
½ **teaspoon pepper**
¼ **teaspoon cinnamon,**
   plus cinnamon
   to taste
1 **chicken, fryer, cut**
   into serving-sized
   pieces
1 **cup uncooked rice**

Combine the olive oil, lemon juice, and spices in a shallow baking pan. Roll the cut-up chicken in the marinade. Bake at 375°F, basting occasionally, until tender when pierced with a fork (approximately 60 minutes).

Meanwhile prepare the rice per the package instructions.

Remove the chicken from the oven and baste again. Sprinkle the rice with cinnamon. Serve the chicken around a bed of rice. The chicken juices may be served in a separate bowl to pour over the rice.

VARIATION: To make **Djaj Mishwi (Grilled Chicken)**, prepare the chicken as above without the cinnamon. Allow to marinate for at least 4 hours or overnight. Grill the chicken over charcoal and serve with **Tum biz-Zayt (Garlic Sauce)**. Dip the chicken pieces in the sauce.

Rabbit with Wine

'Arnab

MAKES 4–6 SERVINGS

1 rabbit, cut into
    pieces
1 cup oil
4–6 small whole
    onions, peeled
¾ cup red wine
¼ cup vinegar
¾ cup water
Salt and pepper
    to taste
Cinnamon to taste

Fry the individual pieces of rabbit in hot oil until golden brown. Place in a covered baking dish. Place the onions on top of the rabbit. Pour the wine, vinegar, water, and seasonings over the rabbit and onions. Simmer on a low flame or in the oven for 1 hour.

NOTE: Serve with plain rice.

Spaghetti with Custard Sauce
Ma'karuni bil-Lahm

MAKES 6–8 SERVINGS

1 pound spaghetti

⅓ cup pine nuts

1 tablespoon butter,
   plus additional
   for pan

1 pound ground beef
   or lamb

⅛ teaspoon cinnamon

⅛ teaspoon allspice

Salt and pepper
   to taste

SAUCE

3 eggs, well beaten

4 cups milk

2 tablespoons
   cornstarch

In a deep pan, completely cover the meat with cold water, add seasonings, bring to boil and remove the zafra (fat curd). Continue simmering until the meat is just tender. Rinse the whole wheat kernels, then add to the meat. Bring to a boil, reduce the heat to medium and stir constantly until it has the consistency of gravy.

Remove from the heat, debone the meat, and return it to the wheat mixture. Mix and serve with plain yogurt.

Crushed Wheat with Meat

Burghul bid-Dfin

MAKES 4 SERVINGS

1½ pounds shank or
  1 pound stew meat,
  cut in chunks
1 large onion, cut in
  chunks
1 tablespoon olive oil
2½ cups water
1 cup burghul #3
1 (15-ounce) can
  garbanzo beans,
  drained
½ teaspoon cinnamon
1½ teaspoons salt

Brown the meat and onions in the oil, then transfer to a pot with water to cover the meat and cook until the meat is almost tender, 30–40 minutes. Remove the zafra (fat curds) as they form.

Cook until the burghul is done and is the consistency of cooked rice, about 20 minutes. (Add additional water if needed.)

NOTE: If stew meat is used, brown the meat and onions in a small amount of oil and continue cooking until almost tender. Proceed as above.

Macaroni Mold

Qalib Ma'karuni

MAKES 6–8 SERVINGS

¾ pound spaghetti

1 tablespoon butter, plus 2 tablespoons

¼ cup breadcrumbs

⅓ cup pine nuts

1 pound ground beef or lamb

1 large onion, finely chopped

2 large cloves garlic, finely chopped

2 (8-ounce) cans tomato sauce

Salt and pepper to taste

Cook the spaghetti in boiling salted water until tender. Thoroughly drain. Generously butter an angel food or a Bundt pan and dust with fine breadcrumbs. Sauté the pine nuts in butter until golden brown. Add the meat, onions, and garlic and continue sautéing until the meat is lightly browned. Add seasonings and tomato sauce. Simmer for 10 minutes.

Place half of the spaghetti in the prepared pan. Layer one half of the meat mixture on top of the spaghetti. Add the remaining spaghetti and top with the meat mixture. Sprinkle with additional breadcrumbs.

Bake at 350°F for 30 minutes. Remove from the oven and let stand in the pan for 5 minutes. Turn onto a platter and leave the mold on for an additional 5 minutes. Remove the mold and serve.

Lamb-Vegetable Casserole
Masbat ad-Darwish

MAKES 6 SERVINGS

1 pound lamb
   shoulder, cut into
   1-inch chunks

2 large potatoes

2 small eggplants, or
   1 large

3 tomatoes

2 zucchinis

2 medium onions

¼ teaspoon cinnamon

Salt and pepper
   to taste

Sauté the lamb until lightly browned. Peel the potatoes and eggplants. Rinse. Cut all of the vegetables in ½-inch slices lengthwise then cut them into ½-inch pieces. Arrange all the ingredients in alternating layers in a 9 x 12-inch pan. Begin with the potatoes, then zucchini, meat, eggplant, tomatoes, and onions last. Sprinkle the seasonings on top. Barely cover with water.

Cover and bake at 375°F for 45–60 minutes or until the vegetables are just tender.

Uncover for the last 10 minutes for browning.

NOTE: This is usually served with rice.

Kibbi

Kibbi is one of the prizes of Lebanese cuisine and is served largely on special occasions. *Kibbi*, colloquial for *kubaybah*, is in fact renowned among all Middle Eastern dishes. The word comes from the verb that means to form into a ball. With the exception of Kibbi bis-Sayniyyi (Baked Kibbi), a ball of the mixture is used in shaping the desired forms; that is, spheres, patties, domes, etc. The basic ingredients for *kibbi* are burghul, or crushed wheat, and meat. Before the days of meat grinders and food processors, the meat was pounded by hand—a process requiring much time and effort. From these two simple ingredients, a variety of gourmet dishes are made. *Kibbi* can be served raw but is most often cooked. If you are preparing a recipe to be served raw, be sure to buy the finest quality meat. *Kibbi* can be served as an entree, an hors d'oeuvre, or as a Lenten or vegetarian dish.

This chapter begins with two basic recipes, one for **Kibbi** and one for **Basic Kibbi Stuffing**. Neither includes serving information because these two recipes will serve as a base for most of the *kibbi* recipes in this chapter.

HINTS

- A leg of lamb is the preferred meat in *kibbi*, but lean beef (such as ground round) may be substituted.

- *Kibbi* should have enough salt when cooked, fried, or baked to prevent it from falling apart in the cooking process.

- For the best results, the ratio of meat to burghul is 1½ to 1.

- When making **Kibbi bis-Sayniyyi**, if there is excessive shrinking from the sides of the pan (½ inch or more), not enough burghul was used. If needed, adjust the amount of burghul.

- When using rinsed burghul that is to be set aside 10–15 minutes, be sure to sprinkle it with salt to prevent it from getting mushy.

- When using *kibbi*, unstuffed, it is best to leave a pocket in the center of the *kibbi* ball so that it will cook through.

- If there is excess *kibbi* or stuffing, *kibbi* may be fried into patties. Excess stuffing may be scrambled with eggs or served on top of hummus.

- Burghul #2 is generally used in most *kibbi* recipes. A personal preference of #1, which is finer, or #3, which is coarser, is left to the cook.

- Burghul #3 is usually preferred for all other dishes.

- When heating frozen *kibbi*, brush or dot the top of the *kibbi* with additional butter for a fresh taste and texture.

- If preparing a recipe that calls for serving the meat raw, it is best to work with a good butcher to assure you get the finest quality meat.

Basic Kibbi

Kibbi

MAKES 8 SERVINGS

2⅔ cups burghul, plus ½ cup when using lamb
1 large onion, grated
2 tablespoon salt
¼ teaspoon pepper
⅛ teaspoon cinnamon
⅛ teaspoon allspice
2 pounds ground lean lamb or beef

Cover the burghul with cold water. Soak for 10 minutes. Drain and press the burghul between the palms of your hands to remove any excess water. Work the onions and spices together with your fingers. Knead the meat and spices thoroughly; add the crushed wheat and continue kneading. Dip your hands in ice water while kneading in order to soften the kibbi (The ingredients must be kept cold). Run the kneaded mixture through a food processor one to three times for a finer consistency.

NOTE: This basic kibbi recipe along with the Basic Kibbi Stuffing (page 120) will serve as the starter for many of the kibbi recipes that follow. When using beef, ¼ teaspoon of ground sweet basil may be added.

Fried Kibbi Patties

Kibbi Miqliyyi

MAKES 4 SERVINGS

½ Basic Kibbi recipe

Shape the meat mixture like hamburger patties and fry in a skillet or place the patties in a buttered or oiled pan and baked at 400°F for 20 minutes or until well browned. Turn the patties once during baking.

Grilled or Barbecued Kibbi

Kibbi Mishwiyyi

MAKES 6–8 SERVINGS

1 Basic Kibbi recipe
1 Basic Kibbi Stuffing recipe, optional

Form two hamburger-sized patties about ½-inch thick with the kibbi. Place a tablespoon of stuffing on the bottom patty. Cup the top patty in your hand and place it over the filling, forming a dome shape. Press the edges of the 2 patties together.

Grill for 15–20 minutes or until cooked through.

NOTE: Other shapes can be made with or without the stuffing.

Basic Kibbi Stuffing

Hashwit al-Kibbi

MAKES 8 SERVINGS

¼ cup pine nuts

2 tablespoons butter

½ pound ground beef
  or lamb

1 medium onion,
  finely chopped

⅛ teaspoon cinnamon

⅛ teaspoon allspice

Salt and pepper
  to taste

Brown the pine nuts in the butter until golden, then add the meat and sauté for 10–12 minutes. Add the onions and spices and cook until the onions are limp. Remove from the heat.

NOTE: This basic kibbi stuffing recipe, along with the basic kibbi recipe, will serve as the starter for many of the kibbi recipes that follow.

Stuffed Kibbi Spheres

Kibbi Mihshiyyi

MAKES 8–10 SERVINGS (3 DOZEN)

½ Basic Kibbi recipe
1 Basic Kibbi Stuffing recipe

Place a walnut-sized chunk of kibbi in the palm of your hand. Using your forefinger, press a hole in the kibbi and begin expanding the hole by rotating your finger and pressing the kibbi against the palm of your hand until the shell is ¼-inch thick. Place a teaspoonful of stuffing into the hole. Carefully close the hole, forming a football-shaped sphere. (Use cold water on your hands to help shape and close the balls.)

Arrange the kibbi spheres in a well-buttered or well-oiled pan and bake at 375°F for 20–30 minutes, turning occasionally until browned.

NOTE: Walnut-sized chunks make about 2-inch spheres. This is a nice size for hors d'oeuvres or for a buffet. For 3–4-inch spheres, use a heaping tablespoon. Other shapes and sizes can be made. Kibbi spheres may also be stuffed with a few pine nuts, sautéed pine nuts with chopped onions, lamb suet pounded with spices and onions, or made hollow without stuffing.

Kibbi in Kishk

Kibbi bil-Kishk

MAKES 8–10 SERVINGS

½ **Basic Kibbi recipe**
1 **Basic Kibbi Stuffing recipe**
1 **medium onion, chopped**
2–3 **cloves garlic, chopped**
¼ **cup butter**
2 **cups kishk**
6–8 **cups water**
Salt and pepper to taste

Form the kibbi into 1-inch football-shaped spheres and stuff. Set aside.

Sauté the onion and garlic in butter in a heavy pan. Gradually add the kishk and sauté in the butter mixture, stirring constantly. Slowly add the water. Bring to a boil, stirring constantly. Add salt and pepper to taste. Cover and simmer for 15 minutes.

Bring to a boil and add the kibbi balls Simmer for an additional 15 minutes. (When thickened, this should be the consistency of medium gravy. Add water if needed.) Serve like stew, allowing 3–4 kibbi balls per serving.

NOTE: Kishk is made from yogurt and burghul that has been ground, fermented, and salted. It has the texture of corn meal and can be found in Middle Eastern shops. Kibbi in Kishk can also be served over rice.

Supreme Lamb Stew with Kibbi

Kibbi Qarnabiyyi

MAKES 10–12 SERVINGS

½ **Basic Kibbi recipe**

1 **Basic Kibbi Stuffing recipe**

STEW

2 **pounds of boned lamb, shank, shoulder, or leg, cubed in 2-inch pieces**

⅛ **teaspoon pepper**

⅛ **teaspoon cinnamon**

⅛ **teaspoon allspice**

2 **large onions, julienned**

1 **(15-ounce) can garbanzo beans, drained**

1½ **cup sesame seed oil (tahini)**

¼ **cup water**

Salt to taste

Juice of 4 lemons (1⅓ cups)

Juice of 2 large grapefruits (⅔ cup)

Form the kibbi into 2–3-inch spherical shapes and stuff. Set aside.

Place the meat and seasonings in a pot. Completely cover with cold water. Cover and cook on a medium flame for about 45 minutes. Add the onions and garbanzo beans, lower to simmer and cook for 10 minutes. Remove from the flame and cool.

Thoroughly mix the sesame seed oil with the water. Add the lemon and grapefruit juice. Blend well with a mixer until it's fluffy like cream. If it's too thick, add a little more water.

Gradually add the sauce to the meat and liquid, stirring constantly. Cook on a medium flame, stirring 2 or 3 times, until it comes to a boil. Then gently add the kibbi spheres so as not to break them. Bring to a boil. Cook 15–20 minutes more.

NOTE: Serve on a bed of plain cooked rice.

Fish Kibbi

Kibbit Samak

MAKES 4–6 SERVINGS

2 cups burghul
1 tablespoon salt
½ cup pine nuts
½ cup oil, plus ⅓ cup, plus ½ cup
2 large onions, julienned
1 medium onion, grated
1 tablespoon ground coriander or ½ bunch of chopped green coriander (1 tablespoon sweet basil may be substituted)
1 orange rind, grated
⅛ teaspoon pepper
1½ pounds boned white fish

Wash the burghul in cold water, squeeze, sprinkle with salt, and set aside.

Sauté the pine nuts in ½ cup of the oil until golden brown. Add the julienned onions and continue sautéing until the onions are limp. Set aside.

Thoroughly mix the grated onion with the coriander, orange rind, and pepper. Grind the raw fish in a food processor. Combine the fish with the onion and coriander mixture. Blend with your fingers. Add the burghul and knead until it's the consistency of dough, dipping your hands in cold water to soften the mixture.

Grease a 9-inch square pan with ½ cup of the oil. Spread a ½-inch layer of fish kibbi on the bottom of the pan. (It is easier to take a large ball, pat it flat, place it in the pan, and piece the kibbi where needed.) Smooth the kibbi out evenly with your hands. Spread the sautéed julienned onions and pine nuts evenly on top of the fish mixture. Place the rest of the kibbi mixture on top of the onions, spreading evenly. Score the top layer ½-inch deep in 1-inch diamond shapes.

Pour the remaining ½ cup of oil evenly over the top and bake in 400°F oven for 35–45 minutes until golden brown.

NOTE: You can fry or bake in a well-oiled pan to make patties. Omit onion and pine nut stuffing.

Baked Kibbi

Kibbi bis-Sayniyyi

MAKES 8–10 SERVINGS

1 Basic Kibbi recipe
1 Basic Kibbi Stuffing
  recipe
½ cup melted butter
Butter

Generously butter a 9 x 12-inch cake pan. Spread a ½-inch layer of kibbi on the bottom of the pan. Leave enough of the kibbi so the top layer will be thicker than the bottom. (It is easier to take several large balls, pat them flat, place them in the pan, patting the kibbi to form an even layer on the bottom of the pan.) Smooth the kibbi out evenly with your hands. Spread the stuffing evenly over the kibbi. Then spread the remaining kibbi mixture on top, using the same method as with the bottom layer. Smooth well.

Score the top layer ½-inch deep in 1-inch diamond shapes. Pour the melted butter over the top. Bake in a 400°F oven for 25 minutes, lower the heat to 300°F, and bake for 20–30 minutes more until golden brown. When serving, cut along the diamond-shaped wedges.

Potato Kibbi

Kibbit Batata bis-Sayniyyi

MAKES 6–8 SERVINGS

1½ cups burghul, #2

2 teaspoons salt

1 tablespoon sweet basil

⅛ teaspoon cinnamon

⅛ teaspoon pepper

1 small onion, grated

4 medium potatoes, cooked and mashed

2 large onions, julienned

⅔ cup oil

Rinse the burghul in cold water, squeeze, sprinkle with salt, and let stand for 20 minutes. Work the seasonings in with the grated onion, then add the potatoes, mixing well. Add the burghul and knead into a soft dough. If need be, moisten your hands in cold water while kneading to prevent sticking. (If the mixture does not stick together, add ¼ cup of flour.)

Place the julienned onions in the bottom of a 9-inch square pan. Cover with ⅓ cup of the oil. Place the potato mixture evenly on top and cut ½-inch deep diamond shapes on the surface. Pour the remaining oil on top and bake at 400°F until golden brown, about 25 minutes.

NOTE: You can use this recipe, omitting the oil and julienned onions, to form patties. Fry the patties in ½-inch of oil or put them in a well-oiled pan and bake.

Potato-Walnut Supreme

Kibbit Batata bij-Jawz

MAKES 2–4 SERVINGS

½ cup burghul, #1

4 medium potatoes, cooked and mashed

¾–1 cup walnuts, finely ground

1 large onion, finely grated

⅛ teaspoon cinnamon

¼ cup chopped mint, parsley, or radishes

Salt and pepper to taste

Cover and soak the burghul in cold water for 15–20 minutes.

Combine the potatoes, walnuts, onions, and seasonings. Drain the burghul by squeezing well and add it to the mixture. Thoroughly mix all the ingredients and grind in a food processor. If the mixture is too firm, add cold water. Knead by hand until the mixture resembles a soft dough.

Place on a platter and score with a fork. Garnish with mint, parsley, or radishes. This dish may be served cold or at room temperature.

Monk's Kibbi

Kibbit ar-Rahib

MAKES 2–4 SERVINGS

1 cup dried lentils

7 cups water

1 medium onion,
coarsely chopped
salt and pepper
to taste

3 tablespoons olive oil

KIBBI

½ cup burghul, #2

2 tablespoons flour

1 small onion, minced

1 teaspoon sweet basil

Salt and pepper
to taste

1 lemon, cut into
wedges

Rinse the lentils, add the water, onions, seasonings, and olive oil. Cover and cook for about 15 minutes.

Rinse the burghul in cold water. Drain by squeezing tightly. Thoroughly mix all the kibbi ingredients except the lemon. The mixture will be sticky but can be formed into 1-inch balls; add more flour if necessary.

Drop the balls gently into the boiling lentil mixture and continue cooking for 15–20 minutes. Serve with lemon wedges.

Pumpkin Kibbi

Kibbit Laqtin

MAKES 8 SERVINGS

2 cups burghul, #1

1 teaspoon salt

1 small onion, grated

1 tablespoon coriander
   seed or ½ bunch of
   fresh coriander

⅛ teaspoon pepper

3 cups mashed, cooked
   fresh pumpkin

⅓ cup flour

⅔ cup oil

2 large onions,
   julienned

Wash the burghul in cold water, squeeze, sprinkle with salt, and set aside.

Mix the onion with the coriander and pepper, then mix well with the cooled, cooked pumpkin. Add the burghul and knead well like dough, adding the flour as needed to hold the ingredients together.

Cover the bottom of a 9-inch square pan with ⅓ cup of the oil and the julienned onions. Pat the burghul mixture on top carefully, then score the top with a 1-inch diamond or square design—make the cuts ¼-inch deep—on the surface. Pour the rest of the oil on top and bake at 400°F for 25–30 minutes until golden brown.

To serve, cut along the lines to the size desired.

Kibbi in Yogurt Sauce

Kibbi bil-Laban

MAKES 8–10 SERVINGS

½ Basic Kibbi recipe,
   makes about ½
   dozen kibbi spheres
1 Basic Kibbi Stuffing
   recipe, optional

SAUCE

2 eggs or 2 tablespoons
   cornstarch dissolved
   in water
2 quarts plain yogurt
2 cups water
1 clove garlic
1 tablespoon dry mint
   or 2 tablespoons
   fresh mint
1½ teaspoons salt
¼ cup butter

Place a walnut-sized chunk of kibbi in the palm of your hand and form it into a football-shaped sphere. If using the optional basic kibbi stuffing, before forming it into a sphere, use your forefinger to press a hole in the kibbi. Expand the hole by rotating your finger and pressing the kibbi against the palm of your hand until the shell is ¼-inch thick. Place a teaspoon of the stuffing into the hole, then carefully close it, forming a football-shaped sphere. Repeat until the kibbi and kibbi stuffing are gone.

Beat the eggs in a saucepan until foamy. Add the yogurt and stir constantly over medium heat for 8–10 minutes. Add the water and continue stirring constantly until the laban comes to a fast boil. Lower the heat and add the kibbi balls—do not stir.

Crush the garlic and mix in the mint and salt. Sauté the mixture in butter for 5–8 minutes. Add the garlic and mint mixture to the yogurt mixture, stirring once gently. Taste for flavor and correct with salt. Continue cooking on medium heat for 15–20 minutes. (The laban will be like thick gravy.)

NOTE: Serve with rice.

Raw Kibbi

Kibbi Nayyi

MAKES 8–10 SERVINGS

1 cup burghul, #1
1 tablespoon salt
⅛ teaspoon pepper
⅛ teaspoon cinnamon
⅛ teaspoon allspice
2 medium onions, grated
1 pound lamb, very lean and freshly butchered, finely ground
Olive oil
Fresh mint or parsley to garnish

Rinse the burghul well and squeeze out the excess water. Sprinkle with salt, toss, cover, and refrigerate for approximately 20–25 minutes.

Work the remaining seasonings into the grated onions with your fingers, then mix the onions into the meat with your hands. Add the chilled burghul to the mixture, kneading well until it's a soft consistency. Dip your hands in cold water to ensure a soft consistency. Grind in a food processor one to three times for a finer consistency.

Spread on a platter. (Spreading is done by pressing and pulling without-stretched fingers to flatten the mixture against the platter. This leaves a pattern of finger imprints in the kibbi.) Olive oil may be poured over the top or served separately in a small container. Garnish with fresh mint or parsley.

NOTE: This is a favorite appetizer and is renowned throughout the Middle East. If the kibbi is to be eaten right away, soak the burghul in ice water for 15 minutes. After squeezing out the excess water, work all the seasonings into the onions. Proceed as above. Add ½ teaspoon of ground sweet basil when beef is substituted.

Mihshi

Mihshi comes from the Arabic verb that means "to stuff," denoting a preparation of food that is stuffed. This section of recipes is dedicated to this category of dish, which is made of meats and vegetables with a simple filling that consists basically of ground meat, rice, and spices.

The vegetables typically used in *mihshi* are grape, cabbage, and Swiss chard leaves. Also included are potatoes, eggplants, green peppers, zucchini, and artichokes. The favorite meats used in mihshi are chicken and lamb or beef ribs. *Mihshi* is a particularly succulent dish with a variety of seasonings that enhance each vegetable or meat used.

HINTS

- In *mihshi* dishes, long grain white rice is preferable.

- Although finely chopped meat is preferred, ground meat may be substituted.

- Shoulder lamb is most commonly used for *mihshi* dishes, but ground chuck may be substituted.

- Of interest: cinnamon is used with all fowl and meats to mask the *zankhit al-lahm* or the particular meaty flavor.

Stuffed Grape Leaves

Mihshi Waraq 'Inab

MAKES 6–8 SERVINGS

1 cup uncooked rice
1 pound lamb
   shoulder, finely
   chopped
⅛ teaspoon cinnamon
⅛ teaspoon allspice
55–65 grape leaves
   (3–4 inches), fresh
   or canned
¼ cup lemon juice
Salt and pepper
   to taste, plus
   1 tablespoon salt

Rinse the rice in cold water and drain. Add all of the ingredients to the rice, with the exception of the grape leaves and lemon juice. Mix well.

Place a bowl of hot water near your work area. Wilt the grape leaves by rinsing them a few times in the hot water. Drain. Place a heaping teaspoon of the filling on the edge of the dull side of a leaf. Begin rolling as for a jellyroll. After the first roll, fold in the ends and continue rolling. The rolled grape leaf should be about ½–¾-inches thick, depending on the size of the leaf.

Place a few leaves in the bottom of a 2½-quart pan to prevent sticking. Arrange the rolls in compact rows and barely cover them with water. Sprinkle a table spoonful of salt on top of the rolls and place a pottery plate over them so the rolls will remain firm and intact. Cover the pan and cook on a medium flame for 15 minutes.

Add the lemon juice, lower the heat and simmer for an additional 15 minutes. Unmold by placing the plate over the pan and inverting.

NOTE: This is especially good with yogurt. If the stuffed grape leaves are barely covered with water, all the water will be absorbed when you're ready to unmold.

NOTE: When using canned grape leaves, rinse thoroughly to remove excess salt.

Stuffed Cabbage Leaves

Mihshi Malfuf

MAKES 6–8 SERVINGS

2 pounds cabbage (1 medium head)

1 cup uncooked rice, long grain

1 pound lamb shoulder, finely chopped

⅛ teaspoon cinnamon

¼ teaspoon allspice

4 large cloves garlic

1 tablespoon dry mint or 2 tablespoons fresh mint

¼ cup lemon juice

Salt and pepper to taste, plus 1 tablespoon

Core and parboil the cabbage until it's limp and easy to roll. Place the cooked cabbage in a colander and separate the leaves. Slice each leaf in half on the rib. If the ribs are large or coarse, slice part of the rib off. Reserve the extra ribs. The leaves should be roughly 4 inches long and 6 inches wide. (They can be other sizes as long as they are uniform.)

Mix the rice, meat, spices, and salt and pepper to taste. Place a tablespoonful on each leaf. Spread the mixture lengthwise along the rib and roll as for a jelly roll. Place a layer of cabbage ribs on the bottom of a medium-sized pot. Gently squeeze each roll prior to placing it in the pot. Dice 3 cloves of garlic.

Arrange the rolls in compact rows in the pot, alternating direction with each row. Sprinkle the garlic between each layer. Cover the rolls with water to ½ inch above the rolls. Sprinkle 1 tablespoon of salt over the top. Then place an overturned heat-proof plate on top of the cabbage rolls so they will not shift during cooking. Cover the pan and cook on a medium flame for 15–18 minutes.

Press the remaining clove of garlic, then mix with the mint and a little salt. Add the lemon juice and mix thoroughly. Pour over the cabbage and simmer for an additional 20 minutes or until the rice is done.

Stuffed Artichoke

'Ardishawki bil-Lahm

MAKES 4 SERVINGS

½ cup pine nuts
1 tablespoon butter
1 pound lamb
   shoulder, finely
   chopped
1 medium onion,
   finely chopped
⅛ teaspoon cinnamon
6–8 young artichokes
½ cup lemon juice
Salt and pepper
   to taste

Sauté the pine nuts in butter until golden brown. Add the meat and sauté together until tender; add the onions and seasonings. Cook until the onion is limp, about 3–5 minutes. Set aside.

Rinse the artichokes. Peel and trim the tough outer leaves. Remove the prickly leaves and hairy center of the artichoke. Stuff with the meat filling and arrange upright in a baking dish.

Cover the artichokes halfway with water and add the lemon juice. Cover and bake at 400°F for 30–35 minutes.

Stuffed Eggplant Supreme

Shaykh al-Mihshi

MAKES 6–8 SERVINGS

1 pound lamb
    shoulder, coarsely
    ground
¼ teaspoon cinnamon
½ cup pine nuts
2 medium onions,
    finely chopped
12 eggplants, 3–5
    inches in length
1–3 tablespoons butter
1 (8-ounce) can
    tomato sauce
Salt and pepper
    to taste

Sauté the meat with the seasonings and pine nuts. Add the onions and continue sautéing until the onions are soft. Set aside.

Peel the eggplants, leaving a short stem. (May be peeled in stripes.) Brown all sides in butter until barely soft. Remove and place on a platter. Make a slit on the side of each eggplant and stuff with 1–2 tablespoons of the filling.

Arrange the stuffed eggplants next to each other in a baking dish. Pour the tomato sauce over the eggplants and barely cover with water. Sprinkle with additional salt. Bake 20–25 minutes at 375°F. Remove the eggplants gently with a spatula onto a platter.

NOTE: Serve with rice.

continued on the next page...

Stuffed Eggplant Supreme cont.

• Use 2 large eggplants, cut in ½-inch rounds. Lightly grease the pan with olive oil. Layer the bottom of the pan with raw eggplant. Put 1–2 tablespoons of filling on each round. If additional filling and eggplant remains, continue layering. Then proceed with the tomato sauce, water, and salt and cooking instructions as above. Cover and bake 40–45 minutes until eggplant is tender.

• **Batinjan Gratin (Eggplants with White Sauce)** is made with béchamel sauce instead of tomato sauce. To make the béchamel sauce, melt 4 tablespoons butter in a saucepan. Stir in 4 tablespoons flour and ½ tablespoon salt. Add 2 cups of milk, all at once. Simmer over a medium flame while stirring the milk until thickened and bubbly. Cook and stir approximately 2 more minutes. Set aside.

• Omit the tomato sauce and water from the recipe for Stuffed Eggplant Supreme and substitute the béchamel sauce to barely cover the eggplants. Bake at 350–375°F until golden brown.

Stuffed Zucchini

Kusa Mihshi

MAKES 6–8 SERVINGS

3 pounds zucchini (12–14 zucchini up to 6 inches in length)

1 small onion, chopped

1 tablespoon butter

1 cup uncooked rice, long grain

1 pound lamb shoulder, finely chopped

⅛ teaspoon cinnamon

1 tablespoon salt, plus 2 teaspoons

3 large tomatoes, peeled and diced, or 1 pound can stewed tomatoes

Pepper to taste

Core the zucchini, leaving ½-inch walls; be careful not to pierce the shell. Rinse the zucchini in cold water and drain. Sauté the onions in butter in a large pan. Rinse and drain the rice. Place in a bowl. Add the meat, cinnamon, 1 tablespoon salt, and pepper; mix well. Then add half of the diced tomatoes to the meat and mix.

Stuff the zucchini three-quarters full of the meat mixture or within an inch of the end (leave room for the rice to expand). Arrange the zucchini over the sautéed onions and pour the rest of the tomatoes on top. Barely cover with water and 2 teaspoons of additional salt.

Cover and cook on a medium flame for about 35 minutes or until the rice is done. Gently remove the zucchini to a serving platter. Serve the liquid in a pitcher. If desired, pour it over the zucchini and filling. Serve 1 to 3 zucchini per person.

VARIATIONS

• To make **Kusa bil-Laban (Stuffed Zucchini in Yogurt)**, use the above recipe, excluding all of the tomatoes. Cook as instructed above. Drain the liquid. Add yogurt sauce for the last 10 minutes and simmer.

• To make **Batinjan Mihshi (Stuffed Eggplants)**, substitute small eggplants (up to 5 inches in length) for the zucchini.

Stuffed Zucchini Supreme

'Ablama

MAKES 6 SERVINGS

¾ **pound lamb shoulder, coarsely ground**

¼ **teaspoon cinnamon**

½ **cup pine nuts**

1 **large onion, finely chopped**

10 **small zucchinis (5 inches in length)**

1–3 **tablespoons butter**

1 **(8-ounce) can tomato sauce**

Salt and pepper to taste

Sauté the meat with the seasonings and pine nuts. Add the onions and continue sautéing until the onions are soft. Set aside.

Trim both ends of each zucchini and wash. Brown the zucchini in butter, turning frequently until they are slightly soft. Remove and place on a platter. Make a slit on the side of each zucchini. Stuff with 1–2 tablespoons of the filling. Arrange the zucchini next to each other in a pan.

Pour the tomato sauce on top and barely cover with water. Sprinkle with additional salt. Bake in the oven at 375°F for 25–30 minutes or until the zucchini are tender.

NOTE: This is usually served with rice.

Stuffed Lamb Ribs and Soup

Dil' Mihshi

MAKES 4–6 SERVINGS

FILLING

1 cup lamb,
   finely diced

½ cup uncooked rice

¼ cup pine nuts

⅛ teaspoon cinnamon

½ teaspoon allspice

1 large tomato, diced

Salt and pepper
   to taste

SOUP

3–4 pounds lamb ribs,
   cut with a pocket

1 tablespoon salt

1 cinnamon stick

½ cup rice

1 small can tomato
   sauce or 2 tomatoes,
   diced

¼ cup parsley,
   chopped

Combine all the ingredients for the filling and loosely fill the pocketed ribs, leaving room for the rice to expand. Skewer or sew the pockets and place them in a large pot or pressure cooker. Cover the meat with water, adding the salt and cinnamon stick. Cover and cook for half an hour.

Add the rice and tomatoes, cooking until the rice is tender and the meat is done, approximately 25–30 minutes. Add the parsley and simmer 15 minutes more.

Remove the ribs from the soup and place them on a platter to serve. Serve the soup for the first course, followed by the ribs.

Stuffed Chicken and Soup

Djaj Mihshi

MAKES 4 SERVINGS

1 roasting chicken

STUFFING
**1½ cups lamb,
   finely diced**
½ cup uncooked rice
¼ cup butter, melted
**⅛ teaspoon cinnamon,
   plus for garnish**
¼ teaspoon allspice
¼ cup pine nuts
**Salt and pepper
   to taste**

SOUP
1 tablespoon salt
1 cinnamon stick
1 cup celery, diced
½ cup uncooked rice
**¼ cup parsley,
   chopped**

Clean the chicken by rubbing it with a small amount of flour on the outside and inside of the cavity. Rinse thoroughly with cold water. Mix all the stuffing ingredients and loosely stuff the chicken, leaving room for the rice to expand. Skewer or sew the opening shut. Place the chicken in a deep pot or pressure cooker. Completely cover the chicken with water, adding the salt and cinnamon stick.

Bring to a boil, reduce the heat and simmer for an hour and a half or until the meat is tender (less if using a pressure cooker). The chicken is considered tender when the meat on the leg separates from the bone.

Skim the zafra (fat curds) from the top of the chicken and the chicken stock when they appear. Add the celery and the rice during the last half hour of cooking. During the last 15 minutes add the parsley.

Remove the chicken from the soup and place it on a platter to carve. Serve the soup for the first course, followed by the chicken. Sprinkle additional cinnamon on the carved chicken and stuffing.

Stuffed Turkey

Habash Mihshi

MAKES 8 SERVINGS

4 cups ground lamb
  or beef

½ cup butter, melted

6–8 cups cooked rice

½ cup pine nuts

½ cup blanched
  almonds, halved

2½ teaspoons salt

1 teaspoon allspice

1 teaspoon pepper

½ teaspoon cinnamon

½ cup water

12–14 pounds turkey

Sauté the ground meat until brown. Add the rest of the ingredients, except the water and the turkey, and continue sautéing for 5 minutes.

Stuff the cavity of the turkey with the mixture. Sew or skewer the openings shut. Place the turkey in a roasting pan with the water and cover.

Bake at 450°F for 1 hour. Lower to 325°F and continue baking for 2 hours or until tender. Remove the cover for the last 15 minutes to brown.

NOTE: You can substitute 1½ cups chopped chestnuts for the pine nuts and almonds.

Stuffed Potatoes

Mihshi Batata

MAKES 6–8 SERVINGS

8 medium potatoes (about 4 inches in length)

¼ cup pine nuts

½ cup butter

1 pound lamb shoulder, finely chopped

1 large onion, finely chopped

⅛ teaspoon cinnamon

1 can tomato sauce or 2 large fresh tomatoes, diced

Salt and pepper to taste

Peel the potatoes; hollow a pocket in each potato leaving 1½-inch walls and a 1-inch opening. Do not pierce the opposite end. Place the potatoes in cold water until ready for use.

Sauté the pine nuts in butter until golden brown. Add the meat and sauté for about 10 minutes. Add the onions and seasonings and cook for a few minutes more. Stuff the potatoes with the meat mixture and arrange the potatoes upright in a baking dish. Pour the tomato sauce, or diced tomatoes, on top of the potatoes. Barely cover with water.

Cover and bake in a 400°F oven for 40–45 minutes or until done.

NOTE: The potatoes may also be arranged upright in a pan and cooked on top of the stove on medium heat, 30–45 minutes. In Lebanon, this is usually served with rice.

Rice Dishes

Rice is an integral part of the Middle Eastern table. Rice is often cooked with vegetables and these combination dishes are usually layered. First the meat is sautéed, then vegetables and rice are added. Then the three layers are inverted onto a serving plate so that the meat is on the top.

The main points to remember when cooking with rice are to use long grain rice; salt the water well to yield fluffy separated rice kernels; and do not stir the rice once the water has evaporated.

Arabic Plain Rice

Riz Mfalfal

MAKES 4 SERVINGS

¼ cup butter
1 cup uncooked rice,
    long grain
2 cups water
1 teaspoon kosher salt

Melt the butter in a saucepan. Rinse the rice in cold water, drain, and add to the butter. Sauté for a few minutes. Add the water and salt.

Cover, bring to a boil, and cook for about 5 minutes. Lower the heat and simmer for 15 minutes. The rice is done when all the water is absorbed, and the kernels are flaky.

Rice with Vermicelli

Riz bish-Sh'iriyyi

MAKES 4 SERVINGS

½ cup vermicelli, about ½ dozen pieces cut into 1–2-inch lengths

¼ cup butter

1 cup uncooked rice, long grain

2½ cups water

1 teaspoon kosher salt

Brown the vermicelli in the butter. Rinse the rice in cold water, drain, and sauté with the vermicelli for a few minutes.

Add the water and salt, cover, and cook for 20 minutes on medium heat, then simmer for 5 minutes. When done, the rice and vermicelli should be tender.

Upside Down Rice

Riz bid-Dfin

MAKES 4 SERVINGS

4 lamb shanks, or beef

1 large onion,
quartered and sliced

2½ cups broth

½ cup butter

⅛ teaspoon allspice

⅛ teaspoon cinnamon

1 (15½-ounce) can
garbanzo beans,
drained

1 cup uncooked rice,
long grain

Salt and pepper
to taste

Cover the shanks and onions with cold water and cook for about 2 hours or until tender. Remove the zafra (fat curds) as they form. Debone and shred the meat. Place the meat back in the pot with the broth, onions, butter, and seasonings.

Add the garbanzo beans and rice. Add salt if needed. Cook for 20–25 minutes on a medium flame until the rice is done and the water is evaporated. Do not stir. Turn the heat off and let stand for 5 minutes.

Turn the pot upside down on a serving platter and let stand for a few minutes before unmolding.

Cauliflower with Rice
Yakhnit al-Qarnabit

MAKES 4 SERVINGS

1 pound lamb
   shoulder, finely
   chopped or ground

1 small onion,
   chopped

1 medium head of
   cauliflower, cut into
   florets

2½–3 cups water

1 cup uncooked rice,
   long grain

1 teaspoon kosher salt

⅛ teaspoon cinnamon

Salt and pepper
   to taste

Sauté the meat. Add the onions and continue sautéing until the onions are limp. Add the cauliflower and water (the water should barely cover the cauliflower). Bring to a boil, add the rice and seasonings, and lower to medium heat. Cover.

Cook until the rice is tender, about 20 minutes. Let stand for a few minutes. Turn the pan upside down onto a platter to unmold.

Spinach with Rice

Sbanikh bir-Riz

MAKES 4 SERVINGS

1 medium onion,
  chopped

2 tablespoons oil or
  butter

1 bunch of fresh
  spinach

2⅓ cups water

1 cup uncooked rice,
  long grain

Salt and pepper
  to taste

Lemon wedges,
  garnish

Sauté the onions with seasonings in the oil until lightly brown.

Wash the spinach and cut coarsely (each leaf in about 3 pieces). Add the spinach to the onions, cover, and cook until the spinach is slightly limp. Add the water, salt and pepper, and rice. Do not stir. Cook for 10 minutes on medium high heat or until the mixture comes to a boil. Then lower the heat and simmer for 15 minutes.

To serve, place a platter on top of the pan and turn it upside down. Let it stand a few minutes to settle. Garnish with lemon.

NOTE: To add a layer of meat, sauté ½ pound of ground beef with the onions. Add the coarsely cut spinach and proceed as above.

Rice with Fava Beans

Ful ma'ar-Riz

MAKES 6–8 SERVINGS

1 pound lamb
   shoulder, cut into
   1-inch squares

½ cup butter

1 medium onion,
   chopped

⅛ teaspoon allspice

1 pound young fresh
   fava beans

4½ cups hot water

2 cups uncooked long
   grain rice

Salt and pepper
   to taste

In a pan, brown the meat in the butter until the redness is gone, stirring constantly. Add the onions and seasonings and continue sautéing. Shell the fava beans; cut the pods into thirds and add to the meat. Cover and let steam for 10 minutes.

Add the hot water and bring the mixture to a boil. Add the rice. Simmer for about 30 minutes or until the rice is done and the water has evaporated.

To serve, place a platter on the pot, invert the pot onto the plate and let stand for a few minutes before removing.

Rice with Chicken Giblets

Riz Ma' Hwahis ad-Djaj

MAKES 6–8 SERVINGS

¼ pound giblets

2 cups uncooked rice, long grain

1 small onion, chopped, optional

½ cup butter

4½ cups chicken broth, or water may be substituted for part of the broth

1 teaspoon allspice

¼ teaspoon cinnamon, plus cinnamon to garnish

1–2 teaspoons salt

½ cup almond halves or chopped walnuts

½ cup seedless raisins

¼ cup pine nuts, browned in butter, optional

Completely cover the giblets with water and boil until tender. Remove the fat curds as they form. Remove the giblets and reserve the broth. Cut the giblets into small pieces and set aside. Meanwhile, rinse the rice in cold water and drain.

In a large pan, sauté the onions in butter until limp. Add the rice and continue sautéing for a few minutes. Measure the giblet broth and add enough chicken broth to equal 4½ cups. Add the seasonings and rice mixture. The giblets mixture should taste salty; adjust accordingly.

Cover, and bring to a boil and cook for 20 minutes on a medium flame. Add the almonds, or chopped walnuts, raisins, and giblets. Stir gently with a fork. Simmer for 10 additional minutes.

Pour onto a flat platter, heaping the rice in the center. Sprinkle with cinnamon and the browned pine nuts, if desired.

NOTE: This is excellent for buffets or parties. If white rice is preferred, omit the allspice and cinnamon. Turkey giblets may be substituted. The top may be garnished with sliced pieces of chicken, then sprinkled with cinnamon.

Rice with Meat

Riz Tajin

MAKES 6–8 SERVINGS

1½ pounds
 lamb, diced
1 large onion, coarsely
 chopped
¼ teaspoon cinnamon
½ cup butter
½ cup pine nuts
2 cups uncooked rice,
 long grain
4 cups boiling water
Salt and pepper
 to taste
Grated cheese

Sauté the meat, onions, and seasonings in the butter until most of the pink is gone from the meat and the onions are translucent but not limp. Add the pine nuts and continue sautéing for 5 minutes. Place the meat mixture in an even layer in a casserole dish or a glass or earthenware baking dish.

Add the rice and cover with the boiling water. Top with grated cheese. Cover and bake at 325°F for 1 hour or until the rice is tender.

Remove and run a knife around the edge of the dish. Turn it upside down onto a serving dish. Let it stand for few minutes before removing the casserole dish.

Vegetarian Dishes

There are many religious holidays, both in the Eastern and the Western churches, which have periods of fasting. Lenten fasting is an integral and important part of the daily lives of the people of the Middle East.

The Eastern Orthodox Church has the following Lenten periods: the Great Lent, 40 days prior to Easter; the Dormition Feast, or the falling asleep of the Blessed Virgin, 15 days; the Christmas Fast, 40 days before Christmas; the Feast of the Holy Apostles, 1 day; the day before Epiphany; the Feast of the Beheading of St. John the Baptist; the Feast of the Elevation of the Holy Cross; and every Wednesday and Friday, with few exceptions during the year. The types of food that can be eaten during these Lenten periods vary. For example, during the Great Lent, there is a gradual withdrawal from meat, to dairy products, to a vegan diet.

The meatless recipes in this section and throughout the book are only a sampling of the foods that are a part of the rich Middle Eastern religious heritage. Of course, these dishes may be used any time of the year as well as on special occasions.

HINTS

• When dicing, chopping, or frying eggplant, always place them in salted cold water so they won't turn dark; eggplant will also take less oil than other vegetables when frying.

• Meatless dishes may be eaten hot or cold.

• When using lemon juice in the recipes, personal preference, desired tartness, will dictate the quantity.

Eggplant Appetizer

Baba Ghanoush

MAKES 4–6 SERVINGS

1 large eggplant
1 clove garlic
4 tablespoons tahini
¼ cup water
¼–½ cup lemon juice, depending upon desired tartness
Salt to taste
Finely chopped parsley and/or pomegranate seeds, garnish

Bake or grill the eggplant until well done. Alternatively, char the eggplant over the open flame of a gas burner, turning frequently. Place the eggplant in a bowl and remove the skin carefully, reserving the liquid. Chop finely.

In the bowl of a food processor, combine the garlic with the salt. Add the tahini and blend thoroughly; slowly add the water, mixing well. Add lemon juice and thoroughly blend. Add the eggplant and pulse 2 or 3 times.

Garnish the edge of the serving dish with parsley, placing a small mound in the center or garnish with pomegranate seeds and chopped parsley.

NOTE: Arabic custom is to pour a small amount of olive oil over the top as well as a sprinkling of sumac.

Eggplant and Garbanzo Stew

Mnazlit Batinjan

MAKES 4–6 SERVINGS

1 large eggplant
1 large onion, chopped
½ cup olive oil
1 (15½-ounce) can
   garbanzo beans,
   drained
3 fresh tomatoes,
   or 1 can whole
   tomatoes, or 1 small
   can of tomato sauce
Salt and pepper
   to taste

Peel the eggplant and cut it into 3-inch wedges. Sauté the onions in the olive oil in a saucepan. Add the garbanzo beans and eggplant. Add the seasonings. Cover and simmer for 15 minutes.

Gently rotate the vegetables a couple of times during cooking by holding the lid tightly on the pan and tossing. Then add the tomatoes and a little water if you're using fresh tomatoes. The liquid should come to half the depth of the vegetables in the pan.

Cook on a medium flame until the eggplant is done, about 20–25 minutes. Serve hot or cold.

Zucchini Stew

Mnazlit Kusa

MAKES 4 SERVINGS

1 medium onion,
   chopped
½ cup olive oil
1 or 2 large zucchinis,
   finely chopped
3 fresh tomatoes,
   diced, or 1 can
   whole tomatoes
2 eggs, lightly beaten
Salt and pepper
   to taste

Sauté the onions in oil in a saucepan. Add the zucchini, tomatoes, and seasonings. Simmer for 15 minutes or until tender.

Add the eggs and stir thoroughly for a couple of minutes until the eggs are set.

NOTE: Both the eggs and the tomatoes are optional.

Spirit of the Cook

Tabbakh Ruhu

MAKES 4–6 SERVINGS

1 pound zucchini
2 large cloves garlic
1 tablespoon dry
   or 2 tablespoons
   fresh mint
¼ cup olive oil
Salt to taste
Pepper to taste

Wash and halve or quarter the zucchini, depending on the size. If too thick, cut in half. Mash the garlic, mint, and salt together.

Layer the garlic mixture with the zucchini in a deep pan. The top layer should be the garlic mixture. Pour the oil over the top layer and season with a little pepper.

Cook on medium heat for 20–25 minutes or until the zucchini is tender.

Sauteed Dandelion Greens

Hindbi Miqliyyi

MAKES 4–6 SERVINGS

2 bunches of
dandelion greens

2 medium onions,
julienned

1 clove garlic,
chopped, optional

2 tablespoons olive oil

1 tablespoon water

Salt to taste

Lemon wedges

Thoroughly clean the greens and cook until they are wilted but not soft, about 5 minutes. Drain, squeezing out the excess moisture, then coarsely chop.

Sauté the onions and garlic in the oil until golden brown. Reserve ⅔ of the onions for the top and mix the rest with the greens. Add the salt and water; cover and simmer for 10 minutes.

Spread the greens on a platter and cover the entire top with the reserved onions. Serve with lemon, which may be squeezed on top before serving or in wedges for individual taste.

Whole Wheat for Memorial Services

Sayniyyat an-Niyaha

MAKES 3 DOZEN

4 pounds whole wheat kernels

1 tablespoon anise seed

1 pound dried garbanzo beans, unsalted and roasted

1 pound powdered sugar

1 pound sugar-coated almonds, white

Silver doilies

Silver decors

Combine the whole wheat and anise seed and completely cover with water. Cook about an hour and a half, until tender. The kernels should not be opened. Drain thoroughly. Spread on a towel until the kernels are dry but tender (6–8 hours).

Process the unsalted and roasted garbanzo beans in the bowl of a food processor until powdery. Sift to remove the large chunks. On a 15 x 22-inch silver tray, cut the silver doilies in half and arrange them around the outside edge of the tray: tape them down. Place rectangular wax paper on the tray overlapping the doilies approximately 1 inch, forming a scalloped design. Spread ⅓ of the whole wheat evenly on the wax paper; gently press down using a piece of wax paper between your hand and the whole wheat. Repeat until all of the whole wheat is used; the rectangle will be compact and slightly rounded on the sides.

Sift the powdered garbanzo beans evenly on top of the whole wheat to generously cover; press down with the waxed paper. The wheat should not show.

About 2 hours before serving, sift powdered sugar on top, covering the powdered garbanzo beans thoroughly. Press down with waxed paper, especially around the edges. Arrange the sugarcoated almonds around the edge of the tray. Make a cross with the silver decors in the center. Using tweezers, press each decor slightly into the sugar in order to hold it. On either side of the cross, place the first and last initial of the deceased with the silver decors.

NOTE: This may be offered in memory of departed persons for the 40-day memorial service, and again at intervals of 3, 6, and 12 months.

Garbanzo Bean Dip

Hummus bit-Tahini

MAKES 4 SERVINGS

1 (15½-ounce) can
   garbanzo beans,
   drained

3 tablespoons tahini

¼–½ cup lemon juice,
   to taste

1 clove garlic

⅛ teaspoon cumin

½ teaspoon kosher salt

Finely chopped parsley
   and/or pomegranate
   seeds, garnish

Olive oil (optional)

Sumac, paprika or
   Aleppo pepper,
   optional for serving

Process all of the ingredients, except for 1 table-spoon of the garbanzo beans, the parsley, olive oil, and sumac, in a food processor and add water to just below the level of the garbanzo beans.

Process, adding additional water as necessary, to form a smooth, thick paste. Garnish the edge of a serving dish with the parsley. Place the hummus in the middle of the dish. Mound the reserved garbanzo beans in the center of the hummus with a few leaves of parsley.

Arabic custom is to pour a small amount of olive oil over the top as well as a sprinkling of sumac.

NOTE: This may be used as an appetizer or as a side dish for a main meal. Serve with Arabic Bread.

Green Bean Stew

Lubyi biz-Zayt

MAKES 4–6 SERVINGS

1 pound fresh green
beans, or frozen

1 large clove garlic,
chopped

1 medium onion,
chopped

¼ cup olive oil

½ cup water

1 (8-ounce) can
tomato sauce

Salt and pepper
to taste

Snip the ends off the beans. Wash and cut into 2-inch lengths.

Sauté the garlic and onion in olive oil. Add the seasonings. Add the beans to the onion mixture, tossing lightly. Cover and steam for 10 minutes, tossing once during the cooking process. Add the water and tomato sauce.

Cover and cook 20–25 minutes.

NOTE: The beans can be served as a side dish or with rice.

Okra with Oil

Bamyi biz-Zayt

MAKES 4 SERVINGS

1 pound young
  whole okra

⅔ cup olive oil

1 medium onion,
  chopped

3 cloves garlic,
  chopped

2 teaspoons coriander
  seed or ½ teaspoon
  ground coriander

1 (8-ounce) can tomato
  sauce

½–¾ cup lemon juice

Salt and pepper to
  taste

Clean the okra with a slightly dampened cloth. Cut off the stems. Sauté in the olive oil until lightly brown. Remove okra and set aside.

Place the oil remaining from the okra in a saucepan and sauté the onions, garlic, and seasonings. Add the okra to the sautéed onions, then add the tomato sauce and enough water to barely cover the okra.

Cook on a medium flame for 20–25 minutes. Add the lemon juice to the okra and simmer for 10 minutes.

NOTE: This is especially good served over plain fluffy rice or vermicelli rice. Frozen okra may be used. If frozen okra is used, no need to sauté the okra.

Tomato Bulgar Pilaf

Burghul bi Banadura

MAKES 4 SERVINGS

1 cup burghul (bulgur
wheat, #2 medium
grind)

1 large onion, chopped

½ red pepper, chopped

1 medium tomato,
chopped

3 tablespoons
tomato paste

3 tablespoons olive oil

1–½ cups water

Salt and pepper
to taste

In a medium saucepan, sauté the onion and optional red peppers until the onion is translucent. Add the diced tomato and sauté until it has completely softened, about 3–4 minutes.

Rinse the bulgur until the water is clear and add to the onion/tomato mixture. Increase the heat and the water and tomato paste. Season to taste with salt and pepper. Stir well and bring to a gentle simmer. Lower the heat and cook covered for approximately 15–20 minutes, or until the water is absorbed, checking occasionally so that the pilaf does not scorch. Once the pilaf is done, allow to rest 5–7 minutes and serve.

NOTE: A delicious variation to make a complete meal is to add a can of drained garbanzo beans with the water. Serve with a salad, olives and assorted pickles.

Fried Vegetables

Khudar Miqliyyi

MAKES 4 SERVINGS

½ head cauliflower
1 large or 2 medium
   zucchinis
1 medium eggplant,
   peeled lengthwise,
   leaving 1-inch strips
   of skin intact
1 large potato, peeled
2–3 tablespoons
   olive oil
2 medium tomatoes
Fresh mint for garnish
Salt

Cut the cauliflower into small florets. Cut the zucchini and eggplant into ½-inch rounds and the potato into ¼-inch rounds. Soak the eggplant in salt water for about 15 minutes, then drain and dry well before frying.

Heat the oil until it's hot. Fry the potatoes until tender and golden brown. Remove them from the frying pan and drain. Continue frying the rest of the vegetables until tender and golden brown. Add more oil to the pan as necessary. Slice the tomatoes and fry just before serving.

Arrange the vegetables in rows on a platter and garnish with sprigs of fresh mint. Salt the entire platter just before serving. Serve hot or cold.

NOTE: This is often served for summer meals or during Lenten season and is especially good accompanied with cucumber-yogurt salad and Arabic bread.

Green Fava Beans

Ful biz-Zayt

MAKES 6–8 SERVINGS

2 pounds fresh and tender fava beans

3 cloves garlic

1 medium onion, chopped

⅛ teaspoon allspice

½ cup olive oil

1 teaspoon coriander seed

½–1 cup water

⅓ cup lemon juice

Salt and pepper to taste

Wash and shell the fava beans. Remove the string from the edges of the pods and discard. Cut the pods into 1-inch lengths. Place the beans and pods in cold water so they will not discolor.

Chop two cloves of the garlic. Sauté the onions, chopped garlic, salt, pepper, and allspice in the oil until lightly browned. Mash the remaining clove of garlic with the coriander seed and add to the onion mixture; sauté for a few more minutes.

Add the drained beans and pods, tossing thoroughly. Add the water and cook on a medium flame for 20–25 minutes or until the beans and pods are almost tender. Add the lemon juice and simmer for 5 minutes.

NOTE: Serve with rice.

Fava Bean Pottage

Ful Imdammas

MAKES 4–6 SERVINGS

2 cups dried
  fava beans
1 clove garlic
½ teaspoon kosher salt
½ cup lemon juice
1 small onion, finely
  chopped
¼ cup olive oil
½ cup parsley, finely
  chopped, garnish
Green onions, garnish
Lemon wedges,
  garnish

Soak the fava beans overnight in cold water. Drain, cover with fresh water, and cook on a low flame until tender, which will take at least an hour. Add water, if necessary, to prevent sticking and to keep the mixture soupy.

In a large bowl, mash the garlic with the salt. Add the lemon juice, mixing well. Add the onions, beans, and liquid, and olive oil. Mix thoroughly.

Garnish with chopped parsley and serve with green onions and lemon wedges. May be served hot or cold.

NOTE: Arabic Bread (page 13) is generally served with this dish.

Fava Bean Patties

Ful Imdammas

MAKES 6–8 SERVINGS

1 pound dried
  fava beans

1 small onion, coarsely
  chopped

2 cloves garlic,
  crushed

1 teaspoon ground
  coriander

¼ teaspoon hot (red)
  pepper, optional

1 teaspoon soda

½ teaspoon cumin

1 tablespoon flour

½ cup oil

Salt and pepper
  to taste

Soak the fava beans in cold water for 3–4 days, changing the water every day. Peel the beans and place them with the onion in the bowl of a food processor. Add the rest of the ingredients, except the oil. Mix well. Process the mixture a second time.

Form the mixture into 2–2½-inch patties and deep fry or pan fry in hot oil.

VARIATIONS

• If you would prefer a mixture of beans, soak ¾ cup of garbanzo beans with the fava beans. Alternatively, this can be made with garbanzo beans only. Soak garbanzo beans for 1–2 days. Then follow the instructions above.

NOTE: Falafel patties are delightful in sandwiches with Arabic Bread or as hors d'oeuvres (make walnut-sized balls and deep fry). They are also delicious in salads with a dressing of tahini sauce.

Egg Omelet

'Ijji

MAKES 4–6 SERVINGS

4 eggs

½ cup milk

⅛ teaspoon cinnamon

1 small onion, finely
  chopped

½ cup parsley, finely
  chopped

2 small green onions,
  finely chopped

¼ cup chopped green
  mint, optional

4 tablespoons oil

Salt and pepper
  to taste

Beat the eggs. Add the milk and continue beating. Mix the seasonings with the onions and work together with your fingers. Add to the eggs along with the parsley, green onions, and mint. Mix well.

Oil a 7 or 8-inch square pan and heat it in the oven. Pour the mixture into the hot pan and bake at 400°F until done, approximately 15 minutes. Check the omelet with a toothpick to determine it's cooked through.

Cut into squares and serve.

NOTE: This may be prepared on top of the stove. Flip the omelet once during cooking.

Cauliflower Omelet
'Ijji Qarnabit

MAKES 4–6 SERVINGS

4 eggs

1 cup milk

⅛ teaspoon cinnamon

2 cups finely grated
cauliflower

⅓ cup finely
chopped onion

3 green onions, with
stems, chopped

½ cup parsley

⅓ cup butter

Salt and pepper
to taste

Beat the eggs and milk thoroughly. Add the seasonings, cauliflower, onions, green onions, and parsley. Mix well.

Melt the butter in a 7 or 8-inch square pan in the oven. Pour the egg mixture in the hot pan and bake at 350°F for about 15–20 minutes or until it is firm.

Cut in squares and serve.

Eggs with Tomatoes

Bayd bil-Banadura

MAKES 4–6 SERVINGS

2 medium ripe
  tomatoes
1 tablespoon butter or
  olive oil
4 eggs
⅛ teaspoon cinnamon
Salt and pepper

Peel and dice the tomatoes. Melt the butter or olive oil in a skillet. Add the tomatoes and simmer for a few minutes.

Meanwhile beat the eggs well; add the seasonings. Pour the eggs over the tomatoes and mix gently.

Cover and cook over low heat for about 10 minutes or until done.

NOTE: Another variation would be to begin with a large, diced potato (cooked or raw). Fry the potato until cooked through and lightly browned, then add the tomatoes. Proceed as above.

Lentils with Rice

Mdardra

MAKES 4–6 SERVINGS

1 cup uncooked lentils

4 cups water

2 large red onions, julienned

½ cup olive oil

1 cup uncooked rice

1 tablespoon kosher salt

Rinse the lentils and add them to the water. Bring to a boil and cook over medium heat for 15 minutes.

Meanwhile sauté the onions in oil until golden brown. Remove the onions from the pan and rinse the frying pan with 2 tablespoons of lentil water. Reserve the onions. Add this residue, the rice, and salt to the lentils. Cook for 20–25 minutes or until the rice and lentils are fluffy.

Place the mdardra on a serving platter and completely cover it with the fried onions. Serve hot or room temperature.

Lentil Pottage

Bayd bil-Banadura

MAKES 4–6 SERVINGS

1 cup dried lentils
4–5 cups water
1 large onion, chopped
2 tablespoons olive oil
⅛ teaspoon pepper
⅛ teaspoon cumin, optional
½ cup uncooked rice
Salt to taste

Rinse the lentils and place them in a pot with the water. Boil for 20 minutes on a medium flame. Sauté the onions in the oil, then add the onions and residue, seasonings, and rice to the lentils. Cover and cook for 20 minutes. Stir occasionally.

Serve on a platter—this thickens as it cools. Serve hot or room temperature.

NOTE: The amount of water needed depends on the heat generated by your stove burners. A gas flame may require a higher quantity of water. Check on the dish mid-way through the cooking time, adding more water in case it becomes too dry prior to the rice being done. Mjadra differs from Mdardra (Lentils with Rice) in that Mjadra is always moist while Mdardra is always dry and flaky.

Lentils with Crushed Wheat

Mjadra bil-Burghul

MAKES 4–6 SERVINGS

1 cup dried lentils
5 cups water
1 large onion, chopped
½ cup olive oil
⅛ teaspoon pepper
⅔ teaspoon kosher salt
⅓ cup burghul, #3

Rinse the lentils and place them in a pan with the water. Cover and bring to a boil; continue boiling for 15 minutes on medium heat. Sauté the onions in the oil. Add the onions and residue, seasonings, and burghul to the lentils. Cover and cook for an additional 25 minutes, stirring occasionally.

Serve in a bowl or on a platter. This thickens as it cools and may be eaten hot or cold.

Vegetarian Stuffed Grape Leaves

Mdardra

MAKES 8 SERVINGS

1½ cups parsley

2 large tomatoes, peeled

½ bunch of green onions

1 small onion

1 cup uncooked rice

½ cup lemon juice

½ cup olive oil

40–50 grape leaves (3–4 inches), fresh or canned

1 tablespoon kosher salt

Finely chop all of the vegetables, except the grape leaves, and mix well. Rinse the rice in cold water and drain. Add the rice, lemon juice, and oil to the vegetables. Mix well.

Place a bowl of hot water near your work area. Wilt the grape leaves by rinsing them a few times in the hot water. Drain. Place a heaping teaspoon of the filling on the edge of the dull side of a leaf. Begin rolling as with a jelly roll. After the first roll, fold in the ends and continue rolling. The rolled grape leaf should be about ½–¾-inches thick, depending on the size of the leaf.

Place a few leaves in the bottom of a 2½-quart pan to prevent sticking. Arrange the rolls in compact rows and barely cover them with water. Sprinkle a tablespoonful of salt on top of the rolls and place a pottery plate over them so the rolls will remain firm and intact. Cover the pan and cook on a medium flame for 15 minutes. Lower the heat and simmer for an additional 15 minutes.

Unmold by placing the plate over the pan and inverting. If any rolls fall out of place, reinsert them.

Stuffed Swiss Chard

Mihshi Waraq Silq

MAKES 6–8 SERVINGS

1 pound Swiss chard

1 (15½-ounce) can garbanzo beans, drained

1 cup parsley, finely chopped

1 bunch of green onions, chopped

1 cup uncooked rice

½ cup lemon juice, plus 2–3 tablespoons

½ cup olive oil

Salt and pepper to taste, plus 1 tablespoon kosher salt

Clean the Swiss chard and wilt it by dipping the leaves in hot water for a second. Slice each leaf in half on the rib. If the rib is thick, remove excess. The leaves should be roughly 6 inches long and 4 inches wide. (However, they can vary.) Set aside 3 or 4 leaves of Swiss chard.

Mix all of the remaining ingredients, except 2–3 teaspoons of lemon juice and 1 tablespoon of salt. Place 1 tablespoon of the filling on each leaf, spreading the filling lengthwise. Roll as for a jelly roll, folding in both ends after the first roll to secure the filling. (The ends may be left open, and the roll given a squeeze before placing in a medium-sized pot or Dutch oven.) The diameter of the roll should be no more than ¾-inch thick. Reserve any liquid left from the filling.

Remove the ribs from the reserved leaves. Layer them on the bottom of the pot. Arrange the stuffed Swiss chard in compact rows over the layer of ribs. (When arranging the rows, work from the outside towards the center, filling empty spaces with smaller rolls. Alternate the direction of the rolls every other row.)

Barely cover the rolls with water and the remaining liquid from the filling. Sprinkle 1 tablespoon of salt over the top. Place a heat-proof pottery plate over the rolls so that they will remain firm and intact.

Cover the pot and cook on a medium flame for 15 minutes. Add an additional 2 or 3 tablespoons of lemon juice and cook for 10 minutes more. Serve hot or cold.

When serving, if there is excess liquid, drain. Unmold by placing a plate over the pan and inverting. If any rolls fall out, reinsert them.

Stuffed Cabbage Leaves in Oil
Mihshi Malfuf biz-Zayt

MAKES 8 SERVINGS

1 large head of white cabbage

1 cup uncooked rice, long grain

1 small onion, finely chopped

½ bunch green onions, finely chopped

1 cup parsley, finely chopped

1 cup olive oil

2 large tomatoes, finely chopped

3 cloves garlic, plus 1 clove

¼ cup dry mint or ½ cup fresh mint, finely chopped

¼ cup lemon juice

Salt and pepper to taste, plus 1 teaspoon kosher salt

Core the cabbage and parboil the head in a large kettle of water just long enough to soften and separate the leaves. Break off the leaves and set them aside to drain. If any cabbage veins are excessively thick, reduce them with a sharp knife. Cover the bottom of a medium sized pot or Dutch oven with the cut-away portion of the cabbage leaves. Cut the large leaves in half along the center vein.

Thoroughly mix the rest of the ingredients with the exception of 1 teaspoon of salt, the garlic, the mint, and lemon juice. Place a generous tablespoon of the mixture on the thicker edge of each leaf. Roll as in a jelly roll. Squeeze the rolls gently when placing them compactly in the pot. Chop 3 cloves of the garlic. Sprinkle the garlic between each layer. The number of layers will depend on the size of the pot.

Mash together the mint, 1 clove of garlic, and 1 teaspoon of salt. Stir in the lemon juice and pour the mixture over the rolled cabbage leaves. Add enough water to cover the rolls. Place a small ovenproof dish on top of the leaves to keep them from separating.

Cover and cook on a medium flame 20–25 minutes, then simmer on a low flame for 15 minutes or until the rice is tender.

Macaroni with Milk

Ma'karuni bil-Halib

MAKES 6–8 SERVINGS

1 pound spaghetti

1 tablespoon butter,
  for pan

4 eggs, well beaten

4 cups milk

1½ teaspoons salt

2 tablespoons fresh
  parsley, finely
  chopped or
  2 teaspoons dried
  parsley

½ cup grated Gruyere
  or Parmesan cheese

Cook the spaghetti in salted boiling water.
Rinse in cold water and place in a buttered
9 x 13-inch pan.

Thoroughly mix the eggs, milk, salt, and
parsley with a fork. Pour it over the spaghetti. Top
with grated cheese.

Bake at 350°F for 25–35 minutes or until the
mixture sets.

Macaroni with Tomato Sauce

Ma'karuni biz-Zayt

MAKES 4–6 SERVINGS

2 cups elbow macaroni

1 medium onion, chopped

2 tablespoons olive oil

2 large cloves garlic

1 teaspoon dried sweet basil

1 teaspoon salt, plus salt and pepper to taste

1 (8-ounce) can tomato sauce

⅛ tablespoon cinnamon

Salt and pepper to taste

Boil the macaroni in salted water until done, about 10 minutes. Drain and rinse in cold water.

In a saucepan, sauté the onions in oil until golden. Mash the garlic and sweet basil with 1 teaspoon salt. Add this mixture to the onion and continue sautéing for another minute. Add the tomato sauce, cinnamon, and salt and pepper to taste.

Bring the sauce to a boil, add the macaroni and heat through. Serve hot.

Macaroni with Tahini Sauce

Ma'karuni bit-Taratur

MAKES 4–6 SERVINGS

2 cups elbow macaroni or ¼ pound spaghetti

1 large clove garlic

¼ teaspoon salt, plus salt and pepper to taste

3 tablespoons tahini

3 tablespoons water

3 tablespoons lemon juice

2 tablespoons parsley, coarsely chopped

Cook the macaroni or spaghetti in salted boiling water.

Mash the garlic and salt in a large bowl. Add the tahini, mixing well. Gradually add the water, blending thoroughly, then add the lemon juice. Blend well.

When the macaroni is cooked, drain and rinse it in cold water. Add the parsley and macaroni to the tahini sauce and toss thoroughly. Add salt and pepper to taste. Serve hot or cold.

Laban (Yogurt) Dishes

Rawbi is the starter culture used for making *laban,* or yogurt. In the Middle East, no home is without *laban,* which is made from goat or cow milk. *Laban* and its derivatives are to the Middle East as milk and cream sauces are to the Western cultures and diets. In Lebanon *laban* is never served with fish.

Laban can be made from skim or whole milk, depending on the preference of the cook. However, for recipes using *laban* as its base, it is best to use whole milk.

Yogurt

Laban

MAKES 8 SERVINGS

½ gallon whole milk
2 tablespoons rawbi, or a starter can be taken from commercial plain yogurt

Pour the milk in a heavy pan and heat on a low flame until it comes to a boil. Remove from the flame. Pour the milk into a serving bowl or jar. Cool to 115°F (or when the little finger can be immersed in the milk to the count of ten).

Using a paper towel, absorb the separated liquid standing on the starter. Stir the starter until it's smooth. Remove the scum from the heated milk. Add the scum plus one additional tablespoon of warm milk to the starter. Blend well. Add the starter mixture to the warm milk and stir.

Cover the bowl with a plate. Place heavy towels completely around the bowl to retain the heat. Let stand in a warm place overnight or for 8 hours. Laban should not be disturbed during this time. Refrigerate for a couple of hours before using.

NOTE: Always save 2 tablespoons of yogurt before using and place in a covered jar as a rawbi (starter) for the next recipe. If the rawbi is from commercial yogurt, the results will be sweeter than a rawbi from yogurt made at home. If the yogurt does not congeal, warm the covered bowl over hot water (not boiling) for 45–60 minutes.

Arabic Cheese

Jibneh

1 gallon whole milk
1 Hansen's Cheese
   Rennet or 1 junket
   tablet
2 tablespoons cold
   water
Salt

Heat the milk to lukewarm in a heavy pan over a low flame. Remove from the heat and keep warm. Dissolve the tablet in the water. Add it to the milk and stir. Cover and let stand for 45 minutes or until it thickens. The cheese is ready when a watery substance appears when cutting into the curd.

Pour the mixture into a cheesecloth-lined colander and let stand until most of the whey has drained away. Then pour it into a 2½-inch-thick round or square pan. Place plastic wrap on top and refrigerate. Drain the water from the pan every day for 2 days. On the third day, sprinkle the mixture with salt, turn it over into another pan, and sprinkle it again; then place it back in the original pan. In a week the cheese will be ready for serving.

NOTE: This is often served with Arabic Bread (page 13).

Preserved Yogurt Cheese Balls
Labneh Makbusi

**1 Labneh recipe
(page 208)
Olive oil**

Drain the Labneh until it's very dry or until it resembles cream cheese. Take a tablespoon of it and put it in the palm of your hand, forming it into a ball the size of a walnut. Repeat until all of the Labneh is used. Place the cheese balls on a plate or tray to dry further several hours.

Pack them gently in sterilized 32-ounce wide mouth canning jars and cover with olive oil. Secure the lid and refrigerate until time of serving. When serving, spoon a small amount of olive oil over the Labneh balls for easier spreading.

NOTE: This spreads well on Arabic Bread or toast.

Yogurt Cheese

Labneh

½ gallon plain yogurt
1 tablespoon
**   kosher salt**

Thoroughly stir the salt into the yogurt. Line a mesh strainer with cheesecloth allowing the excess to hang over the sides and set over a bowl.

Pour the yogurt onto the cheesecloth and fold the cheesecloth ends over the yogurt. Place the bowl in the refrigerator and drain overnight.

When the liquid has drained from the yogurt and the cheese becomes firm, remove it from the bag, place in a bowl, cover, and refrigerate. Ultimately, it should be the consistency of softened cream cheese.

NOTE: Labneh can be successfully made with non-fat to full fat yogurt, preferably Greek-style yogurt. Check the ingredient label to ensure that the yogurt does not contain gelatin, tapioca or other starches which will prevent straining of the liquids.

Cheese Filled Omelet

'Ijji bil-Labneh

MAKES 1–2 SERVINGS

3 eggs
3 tablespoons milk
2 tablespoons butter
2 tablespoons Labneh
    (yogurt cheese)
Salt and pepper
    to taste

Thoroughly beat the eggs with the milk and seasonings.

Melt the butter in a frying pan.

Pour the egg mixture into the pan and cook like an omelet; the bottom should be golden and the top barely cooked. Lower the heat and spread 2 tablespoons of Labneh on the center of the omelet. Carefully fold the omelet in half and cook another minute.

Eggs in Mint Yogurt Sauce

Laban bil-Bayd

MAKES 4–6 SERVINGS

1 clove garlic

1 tablespoon dried
mint, or 3–4 fresh
stems of mint leaves,
discard the stems

1 teaspoon kosher salt

1 tablespoon butter

1 tablespoon
cornstarch

1 cup water

1 quart plain yogurt

6 eggs

Mash the garlic, mint, and salt together, then sauté in the butter. Set aside. Dissolve the cornstarch in the water. Pour in the yogurt and mix well. Place the mixture in a heavy pot on a medium flame and bring to a boil, stirring constantly.

Break the eggs by striking with a knife and dropping them quickly into the boiling yogurt. Cook for 3–5 minutes, then add the sautéed garlic mixture and continue cooking for 15–20 minutes, or until the eggs are hard-boiled.

NOTE: Serve with plain rice.

Cucumber-Yogurt Salad

Khyar bil-Laban

MAKES 4 SERVINGS

1 small clove garlic
1 teaspoon kosher salt
1 tablespoon dry mint,
   or 3–4 fresh stems
   and leaves
1 quart plain yogurt
2 cucumbers

Mash the garlic with the salt and fresh mint (if using dry mint, add below) in a bowl. Add the yogurt, blending well.

Peel and cut the cucumbers in half lengthwise, then slice them in thin half-rounds. Add the cucumbers and the dry mint to the yogurt mixture. Fold together gently.

NOTE: This is especially refreshing in the summer.

Lamb Supreme with Yogurt

Laban 'Ummu

MAKES 6–8 SERVINGS

2 pounds lamb
  shoulder, cut into
  2-inch chunks
5–6 small whole
  onions
1 egg
1 quart plain yogurt
1⅓ cups water
2 cloves garlic,
  crushed
2 tablespoons
  dried mint or
  3 tablespoons fresh
  mint, chopped
1 teaspoon kosher salt
2 tablespoons butter

Barely cover the lamb with water and cook for 30 minutes. Add the onions and continue cooking until the meat is tender.

In a pan, mix the egg, yogurt, and water well. Stir constantly over a medium flame for about 30 minutes. Pour this mixture over the meat and broth and let it simmer, stirring occasionally. Mash the garlic, mint, and salt together. Sauté in butter. Add to the yogurt mixture and cook until it thickens like gravy.

NOTE: Serve over vermicelli rice.

Lamb Shanks with Arabic Croutons

Fatti Mqadim al-Ghanam

MAKES 4–6 SERVINGS

6 lamb shanks

1 stick cinnamon

⅛ teaspoon allspice

1 (15-ounce) can garbanzo beans, drained

1 large onion, quartered

1 large clove garlic

2 medium loaves of Arabic bread, toasted

2 cups plain yogurt

⅓ cup butter, melted

Salt and pepper to taste, plus 1 teaspoon salt

Place the lamb shanks in a deep pot. Cover thoroughly with cold water. Add the seasonings, cover, and cook over medium heat. Remove the fat curd. When the meat is barely tender and a fork pierces meat, add the garbanzo beans and onions.

Mash the garlic and salt in a large bowl. Pour 2 cups of broth from the lamb shank over the garlic and salt, mixing well. Cut the bread into 1½-inch thick pieces. Debone the meat.

In a soup bowl, place 1 layer of meat, followed by a piece of bread, then yogurt. Top with melted butter. If more liquid is desired, add broth.

Stuffed Lamb Delicacies in Yogurt Sauce

Shishbarak

MAKES 8 SERVINGS

½ Arabic Bread dough recipe

FILLING

¼ cup pine nuts

2 tablespoons butter

1 pound finely ground lean lamb

⅛ teaspoon allspice

⅛ teaspoon cinnamon

2 medium onions, finely chopped

Salt and pepper to taste

SAUCE

1 clove garlic

1 tablespoon dry mint or 2 tablespoons fresh mint, finely chopped

1 tablespoon kosher salt

3 tablespoons butter

1 egg

2 cups water

1½ quarts plain yogurt

Sauté the pine nuts in the butter until golden brown. Add the meat and seasonings and sauté until the meat is just browned. Add the onions and sauté for 5 minutes.

Roll the dough until it's ¼-inch thick and cut it into 2-inch rounds. Place a teaspoon of filling in the center of each circle. Fold the circle in half and pinch the edges together. Wrap the ends of what is now a crescent shape around your finger and pinch the dough together. (This looks like a fireman's cap.) Leave these out to dry for about 20 minutes, or preferably, place them in a buttered pan and bake at 350°F for 5 minutes.

For the sauce, mash the garlic, mint, and salt together. Sauté in the butter. Let stand. Beat the egg well with a fork. Add the water and yogurt and mix well. Place the yogurt mixture on a medium flame, stirring constantly for 20–25 minutes or until it's thick like cream.

Carefully add the stuffed pastry and cook for 10 minutes, stirring twice to prevent sticking. Add the mint-garlic mixture and continue cooking for 5 minutes.

Eggplant with Yogurt
Batinjan bil-Laban

MAKES 4–6 SERVINGS

1 large eggplant
½ cup olive oil
1 clove garlic
**1–2 teaspoons
 kosher salt**
1 quart plain yogurt

Peel and slice the eggplant in ½-inch slices. Soak in salt water for 30 minutes, which will prevent the eggplant from turning dark and from absorbing any excess oil when frying. Remove and drain the eggplant on paper towels. Fry in the oil until golden brown on both sides. Cool.

Mash the garlic and salt together. Add the yogurt, mixing well. To serve, place the cooled eggplant on a platter and pour enough yogurt sauce to cover. Or the eggplant and yogurt can be served separately.

Garbanzo Beans with Arabic Croutons

Fatti bil-Hummus

MAKES 4–6 SERVINGS

2 (15½-ounce) cans garbanzo beans

1 large clove garlic

2 medium loaves of Arabic bread, toasted

1½ cups plain yogurt

⅓ cup butter, melted

Salt to taste

Bring the garbanzo beans to a boil, using one can of the bean liquid. Mash the garlic and salt together in a large bowl. Add the hot garbanzo beans and liquid, mixing thoroughly.

Break the bread into 11-inch pieces and layer each piece with yogurt and then the garbanzo mixture. Top with warm melted butter.

NOTE: Although this can be served anytime, it is a favorite for breakfast.

Condiments

Olives and olive oil are essential to the Middle Eastern diet. Olives are served for breakfast, lunch, dinner, *meze* (appetizers), or snacks. My fondest memory is of dipping hot Arabic Bread in the olive oil as it came off my grandparents' presses in Lebanon. Another favorite childhood activity was to roll **Qamaradin (Sheeted Dried Apricots)** and hide it in my pockets for those sweet stolen moments during class when, hopefully, no one was looking.

Crushed Green Olives

Zaytun Marsus

MAKES 1 JAR

1 pound fresh green olives

½ lemon, quartered

¼ cup vinegar

1 or 2 small sticks of dried hot pepper (according to individual taste)

1 teaspoon za'atar, optional

¼ cup oil

2 cups water

Salt to taste, plus 3 tablespoons

Place the olives on a board and crack them with a hammer like with walnuts. The object is to crack the olives so that they open on one or several sides. Place the olives in a bowl with water to cover and soak at room temperature for 24 hours. Drain and salt well, turning them over 4–5 times for another 24 hours.

Pack the olives in a quart jar, adding all of the ingredients. Dissolve the 3 tablespoons of salt in the water and add to the jar, filling it to cover the olives. Close tightly. The olives will be ready in 2–3 weeks.

NOTE: Additional aging increases flavor. If the olives are not well salted, they will become soft. Za'atar is available in Middle Eastern specialty grocery stores.

Spiced Olives

Zaytun Msabbah

MAKES 1 JAR

1 pound fresh green
  olives
2 small sticks of hot
  pepper
3 tablespoons salt
2 cups water

Soak the olives overnight in water. Place all of the ingredients in a jar and fill the jar with water to cover the olives. Seal the jar. The olives will be read in about 5–6 months.

NOTE: To make Mjarrah (Slashed Olive Preserves), cut 4–5 slits into the olives before placing them in jars. Otherwise, follow the same procedure as above.

Grilled Garlic
Tum Mishwi

1–2 heads garlic

Bury the garlic heads in a barbecue's hot ashes for 15–20 minutes. Shell and serve hot.

NOTE: This is a favorite among people in the plains and the mountains of Lebanon…and they never have any colds!

Stuffed Eggplants Preserved in Oil

Batinjan Makbus biz-Zayt

MAKES 1 JAR

**1 dozen Japanese
eggplants, 3–4
inches long**

FILLING

**2 cups walnuts, finely
chopped**

**2 small heads of garlic,
finely ground**

2–4 cups olive oil

Salt to taste

Thoroughly mix the ingredients for the filling and set aside. Wash the eggplants, pull the leaves off, and cut the stems short. Place the eggplants in enough boiling water to cover and cook for about 10–12 minutes until the eggplants are barely soft. Drain and cool. Cut one lengthwise slit in each eggplant, leaving ½-inch uncut at each end to form a pocket.

Place the slit side down and let stand for 4–6 hours (or overnight) to drain. Fill the inside pocket of the eggplant with a tablespoon or more of the filling, pressing it inside. Arrange the eggplants compactly inside quart jars. Place a dish over the opening of each jar.

Turn the jar upside down onto a plate and let drain overnight. Any excess liquid may need to be drained by tipping the neck of the jar. The following day fill the jars with oil (be sure the entire eggplant is well covered). Tightly close the jars. The eggplants will be ready in two weeks. Cut in rounds and serve.

NOTE: This is especially good as an appetizer.

Stuffed Eggplants Pickled in Vinegar

Batinjan Makbus

MAKES 1 JAR

1 dozen Japanese
  eggplants, 3–4
  inches long

FILLING

2 heads of garlic,
  finely chopped

½ cup parsley, finely
  chopped

2 cups red vinegar

1 cup water

Salt to taste

Thoroughly mix the ingredients for the filling and set aside.

Wash the eggplants, pull the leaves off, and cut the stems short. Place the eggplants in enough boiling water to cover and cook for about 10–12 minutes until the eggplants are barely soft. Drain and cool. Cut one lengthwise slit in each eggplant, leaving ½ inch uncut at each end to form a pocket. Place the slit side down and let it stand for 4–6 hours (or overnight) to drain.

Fill the inside pocket of the eggplant with 1–2 teaspoons of the filling, pressing it inside. Arrange the eggplants compactly inside quart jars. Place a dish over the opening of each jar. Turn the jar upside down onto a plate and let drain overnight. Any excess liquid may need to be drained by tipping the neck of the jar.

The following day mix the vinegar and water together. Fill the jars with the brine mixture (be sure the entire eggplant is well covered). Tightly close the jars. The eggplants will be ready in two weeks. Cut in rounds and serve.

Pickled Turnips

Lifit Makbus

1 bunch of young
  small beets
4 pounds turnips,
  sliced or
  quartered salt
1 cup water
2 cups red vinegar

Boil the beets until they're done, about 20–40 minutes. Peel and slice the beets. Wash and trim the turnips. If the turnips are small, make ¼-inch vertical slices halfway through the turnip, or if not, quarter into wedges.

Put the turnips into sterilized quart jars with 1 or 2 beets in each jar. Add 1 teaspoonful of salt to each jar. Mix the water and vinegar and fill each jar to cover the turnips and beets. Seal the jars.

The turnips will be ready in 2–3 weeks.

NOTE: The beets may be eliminated and ½ cup of beet juice may be substituted for half of the water. The beets impart a lovely pink color to the pickled turnips.

Preserving Grape Leaves

Waraq 'Arish Makbus

40–60 grape leaves

Carefully wipe the individual leaves on both sides with a clean towel. Make uniform stacks of leaves with the stem ends on top of each other. Stack from 40–60 leaves, so they may be rolled and placed upright in cooled, sterilized jars.

Place as many rolls upright as possible to make a compact fit. Place a hot sterilized lid on top and seal.

Store in a cool dry place. After opening, contents may be kept refrigerated for 2–4 weeks.

Pickled Cauliflower

Kabis al-Qarnabit

1 large cauliflower
1 cup water
2 cups red vinegar
2 teaspoons salt
4–6 small beets,
   optional

Wash the cauliflower and separate it into florets. Mix the water, vinegar, and salt together. Pack the cauliflower into clean, sterilized jars. Cover with the brine solution.

Add 1 beet to every jar, if desired, and allow to stand for a week before using.

Quince Preserves

Mrabba as-Sfarjal

6–7 cups quince fruit
1 package pectin
5½ cups sugar
¼ cup lemon juice

Wash, peel, and slice the quince in small pieces. Cover two-thirds of the fruit with water and simmer for about 25–35 minutes in a covered pot until done. Cool.

For every 4½ cups of cooked fruit, add 1 package of pectin. Mix well and stir occasionally for 30 minutes. Place the fruit back on the stove and bring to a boil. Add the sugar. When it comes to a hard boil, boil for 3–5 minutes.

Pour the preserves into sterilized jars, to within ½ inch of the top, and seal.

Sheeted Dried Apricots

Qamaradin

2 pounds fresh apricots

½ cup sugar, adjust to desired sweetness

Wash and pit the apricots. Place them in a blender with the sugar and blend.

Pour onto lightly greased cookie sheets, ¼–½-inch thick, cover with cheesecloth, and place in the hot sun for a few days until dry.

The apricots can also be dried in the oven at 250°F for 2–3 hours. Cut and serve in strips.

NOTE: Sheeted qamaradin may be stored in the refrigerator for a long period of time. In the Middle Fast, large strips, covered with water, are placed in a bowl overnight, then eaten with sugar for breakfast.

Dried Apricots

Mish Mish

1 pound fresh apricots

Wash and pit the apricots. Flatten them on a cookie sheet and let them dry in the hot sun for a few days.

Cover with cheesecloth to protect the apricots. Store in the refrigerator.

Fig Conserve

Tin M'aqqad

1 pound dried figs

1–1½ cups sugar, depending on sweetness of figs

1 teaspoon lemon juice

¼ teaspoon powdered mistka (or Arabic gum), optional

1 tablespoon anise seed

1 cup walnuts, coarsely chopped

¼ cup sesame seed

Chop the figs and place them in a pot. Barely cover the figs with water and simmer, stirring occasionally, until soft. Add the sugar and adjust depending on sweetness of figs, lemon juice, mistka, and anise seed and continue simmering. The mixture will be thick and lumpy.

Add the walnuts and sesame seeds. Stir for a minute. Remove from the heat and cool. Store in sterilized jar or container.

Desserts & Beverages

Because traditional Middle Eastern Foods are rich, fruit, which is plentiful year round, is generally served immediately after dinner. Dessert is served later in the evening with coffee either at the dinner table or in the living room.

Some desserts are typical for certain holidays or special occasions. *Mshabbak, awwaymat, sambusik, atayef, zlabyi,* and *ma'karun khishshab* are special Christmas delicacies; atayef and zlabyi might be served in mid-morning or for breakfast. *'Awwaymat* is traditionally served for Epiphany. The well-known *baklava,* as well as *ma'mul, ghraybeh,* and *burma* are Easter specialties, but they are also served throughout the year. *Mighli,* which is made basically from powdered rice and all kinds of spices, is served by the parents and family to guests to celebrate a newborn baby. *Qamhiyyi,* which is made of whole wheat grains, is served with condiments when a baby gets their first tooth.

HINTS

- To draw or clarify butter, bring the butter to a boil, skim the top and place the clear substance in a separate container. The skimmed top and residue may be used in making rice or other dishes.

- Typical seasonings used in desserts are turmeric, saffron, anise, and caraway seeds.

- Rose water and orange blossom water are commonly used instead of vanilla.

- When using syrup, pour cold syrup on warm desserts for best results.

Basic Sugar Syrup

'Itir

MAKES ½ PINT

2 cups sugar

1 cup water

1 teaspoon rose water

A couple drops of
    fresh lemon juice

Combine the sugar, water, and lemon juice in a saucepan. Boil over medium heat for about 10 or 15 minutes or until slightly viscous (220°F). Before removing from the heat, add the rose water and let it come to a boil. Remove from the flame and cool.

NOTE: 'Itir gets its name from a rose geranium. A leaf is boiled in the syrup. Orange blossom flavoring can be substituted for the rose water.

Fried Dough

Zlabyi

MAKES 8–10 SERVINGS

2 cups flour

1 tablespoon vegetable oil, plus more for frying

½ teaspoon salt

1 teaspoon mahlab, finely ground, optional

1 package cake yeast dissolved in ½ cup warm water and 1 tablespoon sugar

1 cup powdered or granulated sugar

Mix the flour, a tablespoon of oil, salt, and mahlab in a bowl. Add the dissolved yeast. Mix together with your hands until the dough becomes smooth. Let the dough rise in a bowl covered with a towel in a warm place for one hour.

Roll the dough until it is ⅛-inch thick on a floured board. Cut the dough into strips, about 2 x 6 inches. Various shapes can be made from the strips, such as a bow, which can be made by pinching the center. Pour 1½-inch of oil in a skillet and heat to 350°F.

Drop the strips into the hot oil and brown them on both sides. Drain on absorbent paper and sprinkle with powdered or granulated sugar while still warm. Serve hot or cold.

NOTE: To test the temperature of the oil, drop a small piece of dough in and if it sizzles and the dough turns brown, the oil is ready.

Layered Pastry
Baklava

2 cups medium
    chopped walnuts, or
    pistachio nuts
⅓ cup sugar
1 tablespoon
    rose water
1 pound filo dough
1 pound clarified
    butter
1 basic sugar syrup
    recipe

Combine the sugar, water, and lemon juice in a saucepan. Boil over medium heat for about 10 or 15 minutes or until slightly viscous (220°F). Before removing from the heat, add the rose water and let it come to a boil. Remove from the flame and cool.

Bake at 300°F until golden brown. Remove from the oven. Spoon cold syrup over each piece until saturated. This will take about 3 applications of syrup per piece.

NOTE: For a variation, spread the filo dough on a buttered 10 x 14-inch baking sheet, brushing each layer with butter. Halfway through the layering, spread the nut mixture in a ½–¾-inch layer. Continue layering the buttered filo on top. Cut in diamond shaped pieces. Bake at 300°F for one hour or until golden brown. Then pour cold syrup over the baklava, making sure the dough is well saturated.

Farina Squares

Namoura

2 tablespoons tahini

4⅔ cups of farina

2½ cups sugar

1 cup clarified butter

2⅓ cups milk

2 teaspoons baking
powder

1 tablespoon
vegetable oil

1 tablespoon
rose water

Blanched almonds or
pine nuts

1½ Basic Sugar Syrup
recipe

Grease two 8-inch square pans with tahini (sesame seed oil). Thoroughly mix the rest of the ingredients, excluding the blanched almonds or pine nuts. Pour the mixture into the pans. Place the whole blanched almonds or pine nuts on the top so that when cut into 1½-inch squares an almond or pine nut will be on each square.

Bake at 350°F until golden brown, approximately 30–45 minutes. Check frequently so as to not get too brown. Cut into squares, like brownies. Spoon cold syrup over the hot squares until all of the syrup is used.

NOTE: Cream of Wheat (28-ounce package), regular, may be substituted for the farina.

A Cake Delight
Sfouf

5 cups flour
1 tablespoon baking powder
¼ teaspoon saffron
1½ cups olive oil
2½ cups sugar
1 tablespoon anise seed, powdered
Blanched almonds

Sift the flour, baking powder, and saffron. Place in a large bowl. Add the oil and rub the mixture well between your palms until flaky. Add the sugar and anise seed; work it between your palms until it's thoroughly mixed. Add enough water to make it slightly softer than pie dough.

Spread the dough gently and evenly in an oiled 9 x 12-inch pan. Cut halfway through the dough in 2-inch diamond shapes. Place a blanched almond on each diamond. Bake at 375°F for 25–30 minutes. Then lower the heat to 200°F and bake until golden brown. Test for doneness with a toothpick.

When serving, cut through on the diagonal lines.

Lebanese Cake with a French Flair

Gateaux

5 eggs, separated
2 cups sugar
1 cup shortening
1½ teaspoons vanilla
1¾ cups milk
3 cups flour
1 teaspoon nutmeg
1½ tablespoons baking
  powder
½ cup chopped nuts
½ cup chopped raisins

Beat the egg yolks until light lemon colored. Cream the sugar and shortening together until light and fluffy. Add the beaten egg yolks, vanilla, and milk. Mix, then sift the dry ingredients together and blend thoroughly into the sugar mixture.

Whip the egg whites until soft peaks are formed. Fold the egg whites into the mixture followed by the nuts and raisins. Pour the batter into a well-greased angel food pan. Bake at 350°F for 1 hour or until a toothpick comes out clean.

Lebanese Cake Doughnuts

Ka'ak

MAKES 7–8 DOZEN

3 eggs
2⅔ cups sugar
1 cup clarified butter
1 cup yogurt
7 cups flour
1 teaspoon
    baking soda
Peel of 1 lemon, grated

Beat the eggs with the grated lemon peel until light and fluffy. Add the sugar, butter, and yogurt. With the palm of your hand blend the ingredients together, pressing against the bottom of the bowl until the sugar no longer has texture. Then gradually add the flour and baking soda to the egg mixture. Continue mixing by hand until the dough is thoroughly blended. A small additional amount of flour may be needed for ease in handling the dough.

Take a walnut-sized piece of dough and roll it into a log ½ inch x 6 inches or the desired length. Shape in a circle, overlap the ends, and pinch together. Place on a barely oiled baking sheet. Bake at 350°F until golden brown on the top and bottom.

NOTE: Sugar, butter, and yogurt may be blended with the eggs with a mixer for a crisp cookie.

Date Crescents

Qras bil-'Ajwi

MAKES 7–8 DOZEN

FILLING

3 cups dates, ground

2 tablespoons butter

½–1 cup walnuts, optional

½ teaspoon orange blossom water, optional

COOKIE

2 cups clarified butter, congealed

¾ cup sugar

½ teaspoon mahlab, finely ground, optional

6 cups flour

½ package cake yeast dissolved in

¾ cup warm water

¾ cup lukewarm milk

Combine the filling ingredients and mix well. Set aside.

Cream the butter, sugar, and mahlab by mixer at medium speed. Add the flour and dissolved yeast and complete the mixing by hand. Gradually add the milk, kneading to a soft dough. Let the dough rest for 1 hour.

Roll the dough into sheets of ¼-inch thickness and cut out into 2-inch rounds. Place a spoonful of filling on half of the round. Fold the top half over, sealing the edges together to make a half moon-shaped cookie. Pinch and seal the edge of each cookie. Prick a design on top with a fork or a malqat, a metal clamp used for decorating cookies: see above. Bake at 350°F for 20–25 minutes until light golden.

NOTE: If a malqat is not available, use a tabi' (a wooden cookie mold) or leave the cookies plain. A malqat is used only on flour dough; a tabi' may be used on either flour or farina dough. These cookies may be kept for 2 weeks in an airtight container.

Rolled Cookies

Qras bis-Samin

MAKES 7–8 DOZEN

5 cups flour

½ teaspoon mahlab, finely ground

1½ cups sugar

½ teaspoon salt

½ teaspoon cloves

½ teaspoon allspice

⅔ cup shortening

⅔ cup clarified butter, at room temperature

½ package cake yeast, dissolved in ¼ cup warm water

½ cup milk

Mix all of the dry ingredients. Add the shortening and rub the dough between your hands; add the butter and continue rubbing.

Make an indentation in the middle of the flour mixture. Add the dissolved yeast and milk. Start mixing and kneading thoroughly from the center. The dough should be soft like pie dough. Cover and set aside for 45 minutes.

Roll the dough into 3-inch rounds about ¼-inch thick. Flute the edge and prick a design on top with a fork, a malqat, or a cookie cutter. Place the rounds on an ungreased cookie sheet. Cover with a cloth and let stand for 30 minutes. Bake at 350°F until golden brown. Let stand until cold. Pack and freeze if desired.

NOTE: If desired, brush the tops of the cookies with beaten egg yolks for a glaze just before baking.

Nut Filled Pastry

Ma'mul

MAKES 6–7 DOZEN

FILLING

3 cups ground
   walnuts, almonds or
   pistachios
1 cup sugar
1 tablespoon
   rose water

COOKIE

2 cups clarified butter,
   congealed
½ cup sugar
4 cups farina or
   Cream of Wheat
2 cups flour
1 cup lukewarm milk
½ cup powdered sugar

Thoroughly mix the filling ingredients with a spoon and set aside.

Cream the butter and sugar until light. Add the flour, working with your hands until the dough is well blended. Gradually add the milk, kneading to a soft dough. Place a walnut-sized chunk of dough in the palm of your hand. Using your forefinger, press and expand the hole in the center of the dough by rotating and pressing the dough against the palm of your hand until the shell is ¼-inch thick and about 3 inches long. Place a teaspoonful of filling into the shell. Carefully close, forming a sphere. Other shapes can be formed or use a tabi', a wooden cookie mold.

Place the spheres on an ungreased baking sheet and bake at 350°F for approximately 20–25 minutes, until the bottoms are light brown. Sift powdered sugar over the cookies while still warm. Let them stand on the baking sheet until completely cooled. Remove.

NOTE: Date filling (page 246) may be substituted. For a softer cookie, add 1 teaspoon yeast to the farina mixture. These cookies may be kept for 2 weeks in an airtight container if placed in a cool place. They also freeze well.

Nut Moons

Sambusik

MAKES 6–7 DOZEN

COOKIE

2 cups clarified butter, congealed

½ cup sugar

1 teaspoon mahlab, finely ground, optional

6 cups flour

⅔ cup milk or water

FILLING

3 cups walnuts, ground

1 cup sugar

1 tablespoon rose water

½ cup powdered sugar

Cream the butter, sugar, and mahlab until light. Add the flour, milk or water and knead by hand until smooth. Roll the dough until it's ¼-inch thick, then cut with a 2-inch round cookie cutter.

Combine the filling ingredients. Place one heaping teaspoon of filling on each round. Fold and close the open edge by pinching with your fingers or a fork. Shape into half-moons.

Lay each cookie on an ungreased baking sheet about 1 inch apart. Bake at 350°F for 20–25 minutes until light brown. Sift powdered sugar over the top while the cookies are still hot.

Suzettes with Filling

Atayef

MAKES 10–12 SERVINGS

SUZETTE DOUGH

2 cups flour

2 eggs

2 tablespoons shortening

½ cup sugar

1 teaspoon salt

1 package cake yeast dissolved in ¼ cup warm water

1¼ cups water

FILLING

1 pound ricotta cheese

1 cup sugar

1 cup clarified butter

1 Basic Sugar Syrup recipe

Combine all of the suzette dough ingredients and blend well. Cover and let rise for 2 hours.

Combine the filling ingredients. Pour 4-inch pancakes on a buttered medium-heated pancake iron or frying pan. Cook until the tops are bubbly. Do not turn over. Place one heaping teaspoon of filling on top of each pancake. Fold in half and press the edges closed.

Arrange on a well-greased baking sheet and brush the tops generously with the butter. Bake at 400°F for about 15 minutes. Spoon syrup, 2 or 3 times, over each suzette, depending on desired sweetness. May be served hot or cold.

NOTE: This is popular for special breakfast. To make the suzettes with a walnut filling, mix 1 cup ground walnuts, ½ cup sugar, and 1 teaspoon rose water.

Biscotti

Qirshali

MAKES 4–5 DOZEN

5 cups flour

1 tablespoon baking powder

1 cup oil

5 eggs

1¼ cups sugar

1 teaspoon vanilla

1 tablespoon anise seed

½ cup white raisins, optional

2 egg yolks, slightly beaten

Sift the flour and baking powder together, add the oil and rub the mixture together with your hands. Beat the eggs and sugar together, then add the vanilla and anise seed. Pour the egg mixture into the flour mixture and work together with your hands. Mix in the raisins. The dough mixture will be sticky. Let it rest for several minutes.

Spread the dough into two slightly greased 9 x 12-inch pans (the dough should be ½-inch thick). Brush the tops with the egg yolks. Bake 30 minutes at 350°F.

Take the biscotti out of the oven and cut them into ½ x 3-inch fingers. Place them on their sides, leaving space between the cookies. Some will need to be transferred into a second pan.

Return to the oven, lower the heat to 300°F, and cook for 20 minutes more until slightly brown. When done, these cookies will be crisp.

Butter Cookies

Ghraybeh

MAKES 2–3 DOZEN

1 cup clarified butter, congealed

1 cup sugar

2–2½ cups flour

1 cup blanched almonds or pine nuts

Thoroughly cream the butter. Add the sugar and continue creaming with a mixer until fluffy (5–10 minutes). Gradually add the flour until the dough no longer sticks to your hands. Work the dough with your hands until smooth. If it's too sticky, add a little more flour. Shape the dough into either an S-shape or ½-inch-thick rounds. Press the center of the round with your thumb and place a blanched almond or pine nut in the center.

Place the cookies on an ungreased baking sheet. Bake in the oven at 300°F for 13–15 minutes. The cookies should be very pale in color. Let them stand for 6 hours or until completely cooled as they are very flaky and will easily fall apart when warm.

NOTE: Gradually add the flour until the dough just comes together; you may not need all of the flour.

Lebanese Macaroons

Ma'karun Khishshab

MAKES 5–6 DOZEN

5 cups flour
1 tablespoon baking
    powder
1½ cups olive oil
1½ cups sugar
1 tablespoon
    anise seed
2 Basic Sugar Syrup
    recipes (page 236)

Sift the flour and baking powder together in a large bowl. Add the oil and rub the dough well between your palms until flaky. Add the sugar and anise seed and continue to work the dough between your palms until it is thoroughly mixed. Add enough water to make it slightly softer than pie dough.

Take a handful of dough and roll it into a ½-inch rope on a slightly floured pastry cloth. Cut into 3–4-inch strips. Gently roll each strip over a solid surface that has a design (such as a colander, sieve, or grater). The cookies will have a pressed design on one side and finger imprints on the other. Place the cookies on an ungreased baking sheet with the pressed design upward. Bake at 375°F for 15–20 minutes until a light golden brown.

Remove the cookies from the baking sheet and while the cookies are still warm, dip each cookie in cold syrup. If all the cookies are not to be used immediately, they can be stored and dipped into hot syrup just before serving. The cookies can be eaten without syrup if desired.

NOTE: Two teaspoons of rose water may be substituted for the anise seed.

Shredded Wheat Pastry

Burma

3 cups chopped
walnuts, pistachio,
or hazel nuts

¾ cup sugar

1 tablespoon
rose water

1 pound burma (or
knafi) dough

1 cup clarified butter

1 Basic Sugar Syrup
recipe

Combine the nuts, sugar, and rose water. Place half of the burma dough on a generously buttered 10 x 14-inch pan, gently pressing the dough over the bottom of the pan.

Brush the top with butter. Spread the nut mixture on top of the dough. Evenly place the remaining dough on top of the nut mixture. Brush generously with butter.

Bake at 300°F for 1 hour or until golden brown. Remove from the oven. While hot, pour cold syrup on the burma. Cut into squares. Serve cold.

NOTE: Burma literally means "round." In the Middle East, it is made into snail and jelly roll shapes by working the burma dough on a large, well-buttered sheet forming a flat compact layer that can be filled and rolled. If burma or knafi dough is unavailable, shredded wheat cereal may be substituted. Slightly crush and layer the cereal instead of the burma dough in a well-buttered pan, then it's ready to use.

Ricotta Cheese Delight

Knafi bij-Jibneh

2 pounds ricotta cheese
1 cup sugar
1 pound burma (or knafi) dough
1 cup clarified butter
1 Basic Sugar Syrup recipe (page 236)

Combine the cheese and sugar. Place half of the burma dough on a generously buttered 10 x 14-inch baking sheet, and gently press the dough over the bottom of the pan.

Brush the top with butter. Spread the cheese mixture on top of the dough and top with the remainder of the dough, spreading evenly and gently. Brush the top generously with butter.

Bake at 300°F for 1 hour or until golden brown. Remove from the oven and, while hot, pour the cold syrup over the top. Serve in squares, hot or cold.

Rice Pudding

Riz bil-Halib

MAKES 6–8 SERVINGS

1 cup white rice
3½ cups water
3 cups milk
1½ cups sugar
   (adjust to desired
   sweetness)
1 tablespoon
   rose water

Wash the rice well, drain, and place in a pot. Add the water, cover, and simmer over a medium flame for 15–20 minutes. Add the milk, stirring constantly.

When it begins to thicken, add the sugar, and rose water. Continue stirring constantly until the rice is soft or well done, the consistency of a cream filling.

Remove from the flame and pour the mixture onto a platter, spreading thinly. Cool and serve alone or with fruit.

Powdered Rice Pudding

Mhallabiyyi

MAKES 6–8 SERVINGS

1 cup powdered rice
4 cups water
3 cups milk
1½ cups sugar
1 tablespoon
   rose or orange
   blossom water

Combine the powdered rice, water, and milk. Cook over a medium flame, stirring constantly until the mixture starts to thicken. Add the sugar, lower the heat, and simmer until thick and it's the consistency of a cream filling, approximately 30 minutes.

Add the rose water, bring it to a fast boil, and remove immediately. Pour onto a platter or into individual bowls. This may be eaten warm or cold but is most commonly eaten cold.

Spiced Rice Pudding

Mighli

MAKES 6–8 SERVINGS

1 cup powdered rice

2 cups sugar

7 cups cold water

1 teaspoon
  caraway seed

1 teaspoon anise seed
  or 2 tablespoons
  bharat (a mixture of
  spices especially for
  mighli)

½ teaspoon cinnamon

½ teaspoon ginger

¼ cup pine nuts,
  blanched almonds,
  and chopped
  walnuts

Combine all of the ingredients, with the exception of the nuts. Cook over a medium flame, stirring constantly until the mixture starts to thicken or is the consistency of a cream filling, about 30–35 minutes.

Pour into bowls. Chill and garnish with the nut mixture before serving.

NOTE: Coconut may be substituted for the nuts. Bharat is available in Middle Eastern specialty stores.

Caramelized Custard

Crème Caramel

MAKES 6 SERVINGS

½ cup sugar, plus
   4 tablespoons
4 eggs
1 teaspoon vanilla
2 cups milk

Caramelize the sugar by placing it in a cast iron skillet over moderate heat and stir constantly until the sugar is melted. When the sugar is the desired tawny color, pour it into a baking dish and quickly coat the sides and bottom with the melted sugar.

Beat the eggs well with the vanilla. Mix the milk with the remaining 4 tablespoons of sugar and add it to the eggs. Pour this mixture over the solidified sugar in a 5-cup baking dish and place the dish in a pan of hot water.

Bake at 350°F until a knife inserted into the custard comes out clean (approximately 45 minutes). Cool. When unmolded, the melted caramel runs down the sides, forming a sauce.

Rosewater Panna Cotta

Panna Cotta ma' Alward

MAKES 8 SERVINGS

1 (¼-ounce package),
   plus 1 teaspoon
   unflavored gelatin
3 cups heavy cream
1 cup whole milk
¼ cup honey
4 teaspoons rosewater,
   more or less to taste

In a small bowl, put 3 tablespoons of water. Sprinkle gelatin over water and set aside to soften. Spray eight 4-ounce ramekins with nonstick cooking spray. Set aside.

In a saucepan, combine the cream, milk, and honey. Bring to a simmer and cook for 2–3 minutes, stirring well to ensure that the honey has completely dissolved. Remove from heat and let cool briefly for about 5 minutes. Pour approximately 1 cup of cream mixture over the gelatin and stir until completely dissolved.

Pour the gelatin mixture into the larger cream mixture, stirring well. Add the rosewater. Fill the ramekins, cover, and refrigerate 4 hours or overnight. To serve and unmold, run a knife around the edges of the ramekin. Place serving place on top and invert, very gently shaking as necessary to ease the dessert from the mold. Serve with fresh fruit or a berry sauce, as desired.

Epiphany Sweet

'Awwaymat

MAKES 10–12 SERVINGS

1 package cake yeast
    dissolved in ½ cup
    warm water and
    1 teaspoon sugar
½ teaspoon salt
1½ cups water
3 cups flour
2 cups vegetable oil
1 basic sugar syrup
    recipe

Add the dissolved yeast, salt, and water to the flour. Mix thoroughly until a smooth dough is formed. Let rise 2–3 hours or until the dough has doubled in size.

Pour the oil into a skillet and heat to 350°F. Take the dough in your left hand and gently squeeze it up between your thumb and forefinger, forming small walnut-sized balls. Using a teaspoon, scoop the balls off your hand and drop them into what should be at least 4 inches of heated oil (350°F).

Fry until golden brown and remove with a slotted spoon. Drain the balls on absorbent paper. Dip the drained balls into cold syrup and place on a platter for serving.

Ice Cream

Buza

MAKES 4 SERVINGS

4 cups milk

3 tablespoons sahlab
(or cornstarch, use
6 tablespoons)

1¼ cups sugar

⅛ teaspoon ground
mistka

Scald the milk and remove it from the heat.
Dissolve the cornstarch in a little cold water and
add it to the milk. Return the milk to the heat,
stirring constantly until it boils, then add the
sugar. Cook until slightly thickened.

Add the ground mistka, stir-ring continuously.
Cool. Pour the mixture into an ice cream maker
and freeze according to the manufacturer's
instructions.

NOTE: Mistka (Arabic gum) is available in
Middle Eastern specialty grocery stores or online.

Cherry Drink

Sharbat

MAKES 1 PINT

1 pound red cherries

1 cup sugar

1–2 tablespoons Basic
Sugar Syrup

Wash, drain, and pit the cherries. Alternate layers
of cherries with ¼-inch layers of sugar in an
enamel, glass, or stainless-steel pan. Let stand 5–6
hours until the sugar has completely drawn the
juice from the cherries.

Drain the liquid into a pan and bring to a full
rolling boil. Store in the refrigerator. This syrup
will keep up to 6 months.

To serve, place 1–2 tablespoons of the syrup in
a tall glass of water with ice.

Spiced Tea with Nuts

Ainar

MAKES 4 SERVINGS

1 tablespoon caraway,
  powder

1 tablespoon
  cinnamon

1 tablespoon
  anise seeds

⅛ teaspoon nutmeg

4–5 cup water

Sugar to taste

Pine nuts, walnuts,
  and blanched
  almonds

Boil the spices in the water for 5–7 minutes. Strain through a fine sieve or gauze.

Into each prepared teacup place 1–2 tablespoons of nuts and sugar to taste; fill the cup with the hot spiced water.

NOTE: This is traditionally served when a baby is born and is always served with a teaspoon. Coconut may be added in addition to the nuts.

Refreshing Yogurt Drink

Laban bis-Sikkar

MAKES 1–2 SERVINGS

1 cup yogurt
½ cup water
1–2 teaspoons sugar
   (adjust to taste)

Place all of the ingredients in a blender and blend on high speed for a few seconds. If a thicker or thinner consistency is desired, adjust the proportion of yogurt and water.

Serve in a tall drinking glass.

NOTE: This is extremely refreshing in the summer. Strawberries, blackberries, and other fruits may be included.

Arabic Coffee

Qahwi

MAKES 1 CUP

1 cup water

1 heaping teaspoon finely powdered coffee

1 teaspoon sugar (or more)

Measure and pour 1 demitasse cup of cold water per person into a coffee pot (or raqwi). For each cup add 1 heaping teaspoon of finely powdered coffee and 1 teaspoon of sugar (depending on desired sweetness).

Place on a medium flame and stir until the ingredients are well mixed. Bring to full rolling boil. As it boils up, foam is formed, and a little froth is spooned into each demitasse cup.

Some households prefer letting the coffee come to a boil three times. After each boil, remove the pot from the heat until the foam recedes. Spoon a little froth into each cup. Repeat the process two more times.

NOTE: Arabic coffee may also have exotic flavoring: either 1 cardamom pod (for 3–4 demitasse cups) is placed in the coffee when it is boiling, or a little urn of rose water is passed around for a drop in the cup.

Arabic coffee is often referred to as "Turkish style coffee" and is not only a treat but also an honor bestowed on the guest by the hostess. Two basic pieces of equipment are required: the small raqwi or coffee pot (a small saucepan would work too) and a tahuni or coffee grinder. Coffee beans are ground fresh at every serving, and coffee is made in small quantities, from 2 to 6 demitasse cups. Finely ground espresso coffee available is a fine substitute.

Arabic coffee is usually served at the end of the meal and when there is company. The coffee is served black and bitter during sad occasions, and sweet during weddings or happy occasions. Most of the time it is served mazbut or "just right."

Afterword
by Leila Habib-Kirske

MY MOTHER WAS A fantastic entertainer. Regardless of party size, she would dress to the hilt and ensure everyone felt welcome. The buffet table was colorful and loaded with a wide variety of foods, as is the way with any Lebanese table. She was often fearless in menu planning. More than once, she would serve beef tongue to an unsuspecting guest. After the initial shock, there were no complaints. My maternal grandmother was a bit quieter, a perfectionist. The recipes in this book were hers, handed down to her from her mother who was a renowned cook in Beirut. She was always in the kitchen, baking bread, making yogurt, and putting up preserves. Both women instilled a love of cooking to me, and I am forever grateful for their guidance.

Bringing this new edition to life was an exciting and moving experience. Preparing recipes to photograph—and retest—brought back memories of cooking in the kitchen with my mother and grandmother. Several dishes were new to me but which have now found a rotation in our kitchen (specifically the **Rice with Fava Beans** and the **Savory Salmon with Spinach**!)

With over 200 classic Lebanese recipes, this book is an encyclopedia of cultural cuisine. In retrospect, this makes perfect sense—my mother was always an academic. It is for this reason that the book takes such care to teach you the basics of Lebanese cooking—in the style that has been in home kitchens for generations. To ignore how Middle Eastern cooking has evolved and has been incorporated into the repertoire of current food trends would be an oversight. Lebanese cooking is flavorful, healthful, and respects the bounty of the garden. It makes judicious use of meats and there are plenty of vegetarian and vegan recipes, suiting a wide variety of tastes. This style of cooking is increasingly popular and Middle Eastern ingredients such as tahini and sumac are increasingly commonplace.

The nature of these recipes allows for customization. Personally, I tend not to stray from the basic recipe but use a heavier hand with spice and a lighter hand with oil. Within my own family, there are strong opinions. During that family weekend of cooking and picture taking, we prepared the eggplant garbanzo bean stew. I insisted on following the recipe to the letter so that the picture would align with the recipe, but my aunt refused to put in the amount of tomato called for. She was so passionate as to say the recipe was wrong and that "your mother knew better." Despite proving my point with the published recipe, my aunt prevailed as she was in control of the stove. We all laughed so hard—almost to the point of tears. And therein lies the nature of this book: it allows the framework for you to enjoy Lebanese cuisine, whether to recreate recipes from your childhood or a favorite restaurant.

Suggested Menus

Meat

Stuffed Zucchini Kusa *Mihshi*

Stuffed Grape Leaves *Mihshi Waraq 'Inab*

Vegetable Salad *Slatat al-Khudar*

Suzettes with Filling *Atayef*

Turkish Coffee

Spiced Olives *Zaytun Msabbab*

Baked Chicken *Djaj Mihshi*

Baked Kibbi *Kibbi bis-Sayniyyi*

Cucumber-Yogurt Salad *Khyar bil-Laban*

Turkish Coffee

Tabbouleh

Baked Chicken *Djaj Mishwi*

Garlic Sauce *Tum biz-Zayt*

Farina Squares *Namoura*

Turkish Coffee

Savory Salmon with Spinach *Samak bis-Sbanikh*

Grilled Kibbi *Kibbi Mishwiyyi*

Tomato Salad *Slatat al-Banadura*

Fresh Fruit

Turkish Coffee

Vegetarian

Cauliflower with Taratur
Qarnabit bit-Tahini
Grilled Fish *Samak Mishwi*
Lebanese Bread Salad *Fattoush*
Fresh Fruit
Turkish Coffee

Crushed Green Olives
Zaytun Marsu
Fried Vegetables *Khudar*
Miqliyyi
Lentil Pottage *Mjadra*
Arabic Bread
Whole Wheat with
Condiments *Qamhiyyi*
Turkish Coffee

Pickled Turnips *Lifit Makbus*
Fish with Rice *Sayyadiyyi*
Green Bean Salad *Lubyi*
Mtabbli
Arabic Bread
Spiced Rice Pudding *Mighli*
Turkish Coffee

Spinach Triangle Pies
Sbanikh bil-'Ajin
Fava Bean Patties *Falafel*
Eggplants with Yogurt
Batinjan bit-Laban
Vegetable Salad *Slatat*
al-Khudar
Ricotta Cheese Delight *Knafi*
bij-Jibneh
Turkish Coffee

Eggplant Salad *Batinjan*
Mtabbal
Baked Fish with Tahini Sauce
Samak bit-Taratur
Potatoes with Taratur Sauce
Batata bit-Tahini
A Cake Delight *Sfouf*
Turkish Coffee

Special Occasions

'Arak

Meat Rolls Supreme *Sambusik bil-Lahm*

Chicken with Vegetables par Excellence *Mlukhiyyi*

Arabic Plain Rice *Riz Mfalfal*

Nut-Filled Pastries *Ma'mul*

Turkish Coffee

'Arak

Brain Appetizer *Nkha'at Mtabbli*

Supreme Lamb Stew with Kibbi *Kibbi Qarnabiyyi*

Triangle Meat Pie *Lahm bil-'Ajin*

Arabic Bread

Powdered Rice Pudding *Mhallabiyyi*

Fresh Fruit

Turkish Coffee

Stuffed Eggplants Preserved in Oil *Batinjan Makbus biz-Zayt*

Garbanzo Bean Dip *Hummus bit-Tahini*

Grilled Kafta *Kafta Mishwiyyi*

Grilled Meat Kabobs *Lahm Mishwi*

Arabic Salad Supreme *Tabbouleh*

Arabic Bread

Assorted Sweets *Mihli*

Turkish Coffee

Glossary of Arabic Terms

This glossary includes the Arabic words for ingredients and utensils used in making the recipes. The colloquial rather than the classical Arabic is used. The final *t* and *yyi* are dropped, as these endings are usually dependent on words that follow or precede them. (See page x for pronunciation.)

Adas:	lentils
'Ajin:	dough
'Ajwi:	dates
'Arabi:	Arabic
'Araq:	anise flavored alcoholic beverage made from grapes
'Ardishawki:	artichoke
'Arish:	see Waraq
'Arnab:	rabbit
Bamyi:	okra
Banadura:	tomatoes
Baqdunis:	parsley
Baklava:	many-layered pastry
Baqli:	purslane
Batata:	potatoes
Batinjan:	eggplants
Bazilla:	peas
Bayd:	eggs
Bharat:	a blend of seasonings
Bizzaq:	snails
Burghul:	crushed wheat; usually comes in fine (#1), medium (#2), and coarse (#3). Cracked wheat or bulgur wheat is not a satisfactory substitute
Burma:	dough that resembles shredded wheat; also referred to as Knafi
Dibs:	carob syrup
Dil':	ribs from meat or leafy vegetables
Daj:	chicken
Farfhin:	purslane; see Baqli
Fasulya:	lima beans

277

Ful:	fava beans
Furn:	term used for Arabic bread made commercially
Habash:	turkey
Halib:	milk
Halyun:	asparagus
Hashwi:	stuffing
Hindbi:	dandelion greens
Hummus:	garbanzo beans or chickpeas
Hwahis:	giblet
'Ijji:	omelet
'Iqdi Safra:	saffron
'Itir:	syrup made with rose geranium leaves. Orange or rose water essences are often substituted.
Kabis:	pickled, preserved; see Makbus
Kafta:	finely ground lean meat
Ka'k:	hard rolls or small cakes, similar to doughnuts
Khali:	vinegar
Khubz:	bread
Khudar:	vegetables, greens
Khyar:	cucumbers
Kibbi:	ground meat with burghul
Kishi:	laban and burghul fermented together, dried and ground
Kizbara:	coriander
Kmaj:	round, flat bread with pocket used for sandwiches, dips, etc.
Knafi:	see Burma
Kusa:	summer squash
Laban:	yogurt or cultured milk
Labneh:	yogurt cheese paste made from drained laban
Lahm:	meat
Laqtin:	a vegetable similar to pumpkin
Laymun Bus Sfayr:	a fruit found in hot climates; flavor can be simulated by combining one-part grapefruit juice and two parts lemon juice
Lifit:	turnips
Lsanat:	tongues
Lubyi:	green beans

Lubyi:	Msallat black-eyed peas
Mahlab:	a seasoning used in dough or pastries.
Ma'karuni:	refers to pastas (spaghetti and macaroni)
Makbus:	pickled, preserved (in vinegar or oil)
Malfuf:	cabbage
Malqat:	metal clamp used in decorating (by pinching) cookies
Marquq:	very thin, round, flat bread, rolled like Italian pizza dough
Mazahir:	orange blossom essence
Maward:	rose water
Mawzat:	meat shanks
Mdaqa:	large wooden mallet
Meze:	appetizers or hors d'oeuvres
Mihli:	assorted sweets made with filo dough
Mihshi:	stuffed meats or vegetables
Miqli:	fried
Mish Mish:	apricots
Mishwi:	grilled
Mistka:	Arabic gum, commonly referred to as mustica
Mlabbas:	sugar-coated almonds
Mlukhiyyi:	green leafy vegetable, known also as "Jew's mallow"
Mnazli:	stew; refers to dishes made with eggplants or other vegetables as the basic ingredient
Makanek:	sausage
Mrabba:	jam
Na'na':	mint
Nayyi:	raw
Nkha'at:	brains, lamb or beef
Qarnabit:	cauliflower
Qasbi:	liver
Qdami:	roasted and unsalted garbanzo beans
Raqwi:	Arabic coffee pot
Rawbi:	a starter or culture for making yogurt
Riz:	rice
Sahlab:	a flour made from the tuber of orchid genus Orchis; cornstarch may be substituted at double the quantity
Saj:	paper-thin bread that is baked over a metal dome on an open fire

GLOSSARY OF ARABIC TERMS

Salsa:	sauce
Samak:	fish
Samni:	the Middle East equivalent of butter
Sanamura:	herring
Sayniyyi:	pan
Sbanikh:	spinach
Sfarjal:	quince
Sharbat:	beverages
Sh'iriyyi:	vermicelli
Shurbat:	soup
Sikkar:	sugar
Silq:	Swiss chard
Sumac:	tart, ground seasoning from seed of sumac tree
Siyami:	Lenten
Slata:	salad
Smid:	grain similar to regular Cream of Wheat, semolina, or farina; used for cake and filled-cookie dough
Tabi':	wooden cookie mold
Tahini:	heavy sesame seed oil (not the type used in Oriental cooking)
Tahuni:	coffee grinder
Taratur:	tahini sauce
Tin:	figs
Tlami:	round, flat, soft-textured bread without pocket used for *mnaqish and as regular bread*
Tum:	garlic
Waraq:	leaves used in mihshi; such as grape.
Waraq Silq:	Swiss chard leaves
Yakhni:	stew; refers to dishes made with potatoes as the main ingredient
Zafra:	meat curds appearing when cooking meat in water
Za'atar:	plant found in the Middle East; also refers to a seasoning blended from za'atar, thyme, marjoram, sumac, and salt
Zankha:	a special "meaty" smell or feel associated with uncooked meat
Zayt:	oil
Zaytun:	olives

LEBANESE CUISINE

Index of Recipes

Z

About the Authors

DR. MADELAIN FARAH WROTE the original edition of *Lebanese Cuisine* in 1972 to memorialize the recipes her mother had passed down and share these unique creations with the world. Author of many books including *Marriage and Sexuality in Islam* and *Pocket Bread Potpourri*, Dr. Farah was a woman of many gifts: teacher, linguist, writer, Fulbright scholar, former model and beauty queen. Among her extensive academic accomplishments is a doctorate from the University of Utah in Middle East studies, sociology, and language and literature. Dr. Farah was also an educator who spent a number of years teaching French and lecturing with an emphasis on Middle East culture and literature.

LEILA HABIB-KIRSKE HAS LONG been passionate about her Lebanese background and sharing her love of Lebanese cuisine with a broader audience. A financial executive in the technology industry and an advanced home cook, she grew up in the kitchen of her mother and grandmother as an avid taster and assistant. Through them (as well as her own experiences with international travel), she learned Lebanese and Moroccan cooking using traditional methods and has crafted new recipes of her own. She is also an analog film photographer and enjoys traveling, particularly through Europe and Northern Africa, which informs her flavor profiles.